BEYOND THE TITLE

BUILDING AN EXECUTIVE BRAND
TO INSPIRE, INFLUENCE, AND
ADVANCE YOUR CAREER

Beyond The Title
By: Martin Rowinski
www.MartinRowinski.com

Copyright © 2025 by Ultimate Publishing House

All rights reserved. No part of this book may be reproduced in any form or by any means without written permission from the publisher. For permission inquiries, please contact:

Attention: Permissions Coordinator
Ultimate Publishing House 205 Glen Shields Avenue Toronto, Ontario, Canada L4K 1T3
Email: info@ultimatepublishinghouse.com

Ultimate Publishing House – Bulk Orders & Corporate Gifting

Looking to elevate your brand or inspire your team? Bulk copies of Beyond The Title are available for companies, organizations, educational institutions, conferences, and client gifting.

Special Incentive for Bulk Orders:
- ✓ Orders of **100 copies or more** qualify for special pricing.
- ✓ Orders of **1,000 copies or more** receive deep volume discounts **plus a complimentary custom second page** featuring your logo, message from the CEO, or brand story — turning this book into a powerful branded asset or client gift.

Whether you're using it for leadership retreats, onboarding, holiday gifts, sponsorship bonuses, or brand awareness campaigns, this book becomes **your voice in their hands.**

To place a custom bulk order or to discuss tailored publishing solutions:
Call Ultimate Publishing House: 647-883-1758
www.ultimatepublishinghouse.com
Email: info@ultimatepublishinghouse.com

BEYOND THE TITLE BY: MARTIN ROWINSKI
Bestselling Author · Leadership Strategist · Technology Innovator

ISBN: 979-8-9882088-8-4

FOREWORD

In leadership and life, your brand is everything. Each day of our journey through life, we surround ourselves with brands. What makes us select one brand of coffee over another, one brand of cereal, of beverage, of automobile? We live each day of our life in a selection process, choosing the brands that most satisfy our needs. We select those brands based on several criteria. First might be the external appearance or packaging. Most important, however, is what's inside. Of paramount importance is the question of trust. Can we count on that product to perform, day in and day out, with quality and integrity.

We recognize that the success of product brands or even corporate identities are forms of differentiation. Why then, do we pay so little attention to our own differentiation, our own personal brand? Why do we allow others to put a brand on us, rather than each of us determining our own identity and working each day to perfect that brand reputation? Just like a consumer product on the shelf, we must differentiate ourselves to those around us.

Too often we let a title define our brand. You're an "accountant", or a "marketing specialist" and suddenly you find yourself in a box. When opportunities arise, you're now labeled and deemed inappropriate for the next opportunity. Perhaps you find it difficult to think "ouside of the box". Well here's the secret, as clearly outlined in Martin Rowinski's Beyond the Title. There is no "box"! Our own perception of our role, our job, or even our identity is often self-imposed. We others, or even titles, to establish our identity and that identity can become a box, constraining our opportunity and our upward potential.

Yes, we all have titles in a traditional corporate hierarchy, but do you wish to have your identity be defined as a role...or as a leader? A leader isn't constrained by any given specialty. A leader must have a broad knowledge of all aspects of a business to effectively lead those of various skills. But how do we establish those leadership qualities and build that reputation as a leader versus a manager? As you'll find in the pages that follow, there are many steps you can take. From establishing thought leadership, to crafting your own brand narrative, there is one common denominator among all leaders. They learn to learn.

Learning happens when we step outside of our comfort zone. Within your area of expertise, you will have deep knowledge. It is when you step outside of that box, into a new role, that your learning begins. Seldom does an "operations" person raise their hand to ask for a role in "finance", or vice versa. Yet, an operations person with a practical understanding of the financial role will ultimately make a better senior executive. Throughout my own career, I made those shifts from one side of the business to the next. When it came time to select a CEO to lead 7-Eleven, I was a strong candidate for the job after serving in every chair from store operations to marketing to CFO and ultimately COO and finally CEO. Each of those titles was a step along the way but none of them defined my personal "brand". Throughout my leadership journey, I sought to build a brand that defined me as a "leader".

The final, and perhaps most important, element to establishing a personal brand is one's character. Who would you prefer to work with, someone with personal attributes like integrity, compassion, gratitude, humility and confidence...or someone who is untrustworthy and presents a victim mentality. Of course you would prefer the former. We sometimes forget that our character represents the absolute foundation of our personal brand, our leadership style and our ultimate success. Losers and liars can enjoy short term wins, but sustainable leadership success requires a solid foundation of character. These attributes aren't one-time skills but instead must be perfected every day of one's career, and certainly one's life.

In fact, corporate leadership is like life itself. The more we perfect our personal identy, the more success and peronal fulfillment we can enjoy. Read on...and let your learning journey continue!.

>—James W. Keyes
> Former CEO 7-Eleven, Chairman & CEO, Blockbuster, and author of *Education is Freedom: The Future is In Your Hands*

ACKNOWLEDGEMENTS

What began as a simple personal project—an idea to define my own executive brand—quickly evolved into something far greater than I ever imagined. What started as reflection became passion. That passion became a mission: to help other leaders realize their own value, define their narrative, and build a legacy that reaches far beyond the title they hold.

Over time, executive branding became not just part of my journey—but a core element of how we serve leaders through Boardsi. From writing compelling biographies and thought leadership articles featured on **LEADAFI**, to in-depth interviews on the *Boardsi Leadership Talks* podcast, and now, with this book, I've had the privilege of helping others tell their story, amplify their voice, and elevate their impact.

This book would not have been possible without the unwavering faith and support that's surrounded me from the very beginning.

First and foremost, I am deeply grateful to **God**, who has been my strength, my guidance, and my constant through every chapter of life—both in business and beyond.

To my wife and best friend, **Emmy**—thank you for standing beside me in every season, through the good times and the challenges. Your love, support, and belief in me have made all the difference.

To my incredible children, **Daren and Samantha**—I could not be more proud of the leaders and entrepreneurs you're becoming. Watching you grow into your own path has been one of the greatest joys of my life.

To my publisher and dear friend, Felicia Pizzonia of Ultimate Publishing House — the visionary and IP creator behind the titles *Corporate Matchmaker* and *Beyond the Title,* thank you for your creative ability and goodness.

To my **friends,** thank you for your continued support and encouragement. Your presence reminds me that success is always a shared journey.

And to my business **partners—Cameron, Daniel, Richard, Erik, and Luke**—thank you for believing in the vision, contributing your expertise, and helping push the boundaries of what's possible. Your partnership has been instrumental in bringing Boardsi—and this book—to life.

To every executive who has trusted us with their brand, their voice, and their legacy—thank you. This book is for you. Keep building. Keep leading. Keep reaching beyond the title.

— Martin Rowinski

CONTENTS

CHAPTER 1: INTRODUCTION TO EXECUTIVE BRANDING 1
    Content Overview. 2
    What Is Executive Branding? 3
    Why Executive Branding Matters 4
    The Evolution of Personal Branding 5
    Why Now? The Urgency of Executive Branding in Today's Business World. . . 9

CHAPTER 2: THE COMPONENTS OF EXECUTIVE BRANDING . . 11
    Essential Components Summary 12
    Strategies to Boost Your Visibility. 16
    Strategies for Establishing and Sustaining a Robust Reputation 19
    Unifying Everything. 21

CHAPTER 3: IDENTIFYING YOUR UNIQUE
VALUE PROPOSITION 23
    An Insight into Self-Assessment Tools 24
    Understanding the Unique Value Proposition. 24
    Identifying Your UVP: Self-Assessment Tools and Techniques 24
    Aligning Your UVP with Organizational Goals 26
    A Thoughtfully Designed Unique Value Proposition 27
    Optimizing Your Unique Value Proposition 34
    UVP Worksheet 49

CHAPTER 4: CRAFTING YOUR EXECUTIVE BRAND NARRATIVE . . 55
  The Art of Storytelling in Executive Branding. 56

CHAPTER 5: BUILDING AN ONLINE PRESENCE 73
  The Importance of a Strong Online Presence for Executives 74
  1. Profile Image and Background Image 78

CHAPTER 5B: HOW TO USE AI WITH LINKEDIN AUTHENTICALLY - BY JOE APFELBAUM CEO OF EVYAI. 93
  Why LinkedIn Matters 94
  Your LinkedIn Profile: More Important Than Your Website. 95
  Crafting the Perfect Connection Note 95
  Expanding Your Network. 96
  What's Next After Adding Connections?. 96
  AI-Powered Posting. 97
  Join the Community 97
  How Often Should You Post on LinkedIn?. 97
  Leveraging AI to Enhance Your LinkedIn Presence. 98
  Strategies to Increase Engagement on LinkedIn 99
  Building Relationships Through Direct Messaging 99
  Optimizing Your LinkedIn Profile. 100

CHAPTER 6: NETWORKING AND RELATIONSHIP BUILDING. . . 103
  The Importance of Networking in Executive Branding. 104
  Why Networking is Essential for Executives. 104
  Effective Networking: Beyond Collecting Contacts. 107
  Networking as a Foundation for Influence and Leadership 110
  Final Thoughts on Networking for Executives 112
  2. Strategies for In-Person Networking. 112

CHAPTER 7: THOUGHT LEADERSHIP AND CONTENT CREATION. 131
  The Importance of Thought Leadership for Executives 132
  Getting Featured on Established Podcasts. 135
  Why Public Speaking Matters for Executives 150
  Tools for Thought Leadership and Content Creation 160
  Putting It All Together: Building Your Thought Leadership Toolkit 166

CHAPTER 8: LEVERAGING PUBLIC SPEAKING AND MEDIA APPEARANCES........................169
    The Power of Public Speaking and Media Engagements for Executive Branding170
    Why Public Speaking and Media Engagements Matter for Executives......170
    Chapter Wrap-Up...................................194

CHAPTER 9: MANAGING YOUR REPUTATION...........197
    Why Reputation Management Matters for Executives..............198
    Techniques for Monitoring Your Reputation...................199
    Responding to Criticism and Negative Feedback.................201
    Leveraging Positive Testimonials and Building Trust.............203
    Leveraging a Google Knowledge Panel for Executive Branding and Reputation Management....................................206
    Why a Google Knowledge Panel Matters for Executives............206
    Benefits of a Google Knowledge Panel for Reputation Management.....207
    Steps to Qualify for and Optimize Your Google Knowledge Panel......208
    Making the Most of Your Google Knowledge Panel................211

CHAPTER 10: NAVIGATING CHALLENGES AND CRISIS MANAGEMENT..................................213
    Why Crisis Management Matters for Executives................214
    Proactive Crisis Management Strategies....................217
    Responding to the Crisis in Real-Time.....................219
    Learning from Real-Life Case Studies.....................221
    Turning Crises into Opportunities for Positive Change............223

CHAPTER 11: MEASURING YOUR EXECUTIVE BRAND IMPACT 227
    Why Measuring Your Brand Impact is Essential................228
    Tools for Measuring Brand Impact.......................237
    Refining Your Brand Strategy Based on Results................239
    Conclusion.....................................242

CHAPTER 12: THE ROLE OF MENTORSHIP IN EXECUTIVE BRANDING.....................................245
    Why Mentorship is Essential for Executive Branding.............246
    The Benefits of Mentorship in Expanding Your Professional Network....247
    Mentorship as a Showcase of Leadership and Expertise............248
    The Value of Continuous Learning Through Mentorship............249
    Case Study: How Mentorship Enhanced an Executive Brand.........249
    Practical Steps for Engaging in Mentorship..................250

CHAPTER 13: ALIGNING YOUR EXECUTIVE BRAND WITH CORPORATE CULTURE 253

Why Aligning Your Brand with Corporate Culture Matters 254
Strategies for Aligning Your Executive Brand with Corporate Culture. 255
The Impact of Brand-Corporate Alignment on Corporate Cohesion. 258
Practical Steps for Aligning Your Brand with Corporate Culture 259

CHAPTER 14: THE LONG-TERM MAINTENANCE OF AN EXECUTIVE BRAND 263

Why Long-Term Brand Maintenance Matters 264
Key Strategies for Sustaining an Executive Brand. 265
Practical Steps for Long-Term Brand Maintenance. 269

CHAPTER 15: FUTURE TRENDS IN EXECUTIVE BRANDING. . . 273

The Impact of Technology on Executive Branding 274
Navigating the Remote Work Era 275
Embracing Diversity, Equity, and Inclusion (DEI) as Core Brand Values . . .275
The Rise of Personalization and Human-Centered Branding 276
Sustainability and Social Impact as Brand Differentiators 276
Proactively Preparing for Crisis Management. 277
Keeping Your Executive Brand Agile and Future-Focused 278
Practical Steps to Embrace Future Trends in Executive Branding 278
Conclusion: Staying Future-Ready with a Proactive Brand 279

CHAPTER 16: TAKE ACTION TODAY - CRAFTING YOUR LEADERSHIP LEGACY THROUGH WRITING 281

1. Develop Titles That Capture Your Core Message. 282
2. Let Your Values Guide the Narrative. 282
3. Write With Impact Using Suggested Titles .283
4. Share and Amplify Your Voice. 285

FINAL THOUGHTS: YOUR BRAND, YOUR LEGACY 287

RECOMMENDED RESOURCES FOR EXECUTIVES 289

Boardsi 290
Ultimate Publishing House. 291
LEADAFI 292
7 Wonders Podcast 292
Brand Alchemy. 293
GLDN PR. 293

UNLOCK THE MAGIC—
SCAN, TO LEARN MORE!

INTRODUCTION TO EXECUTIVE BRANDING

CONTENT OVERVIEW

In an age defined by rapid technological advancements, intense global competition, and a constantly evolving corporate landscape, distinguishing oneself as an executive has become more critical than ever. Executive branding is far more than a mere trend; it is a strategic tool that not only enhances a professional's career but also fortifies their reputation and expands their influence—both within their organization and across the broader industry.

This chapter delves into the fundamental principles of executive branding, highlighting its significance and underscoring its indispensable role in helping leaders thrive in today's competitive business environment. Additionally, we will examine the evolution of personal branding, exploring its profound implications for career progression and organizational success.

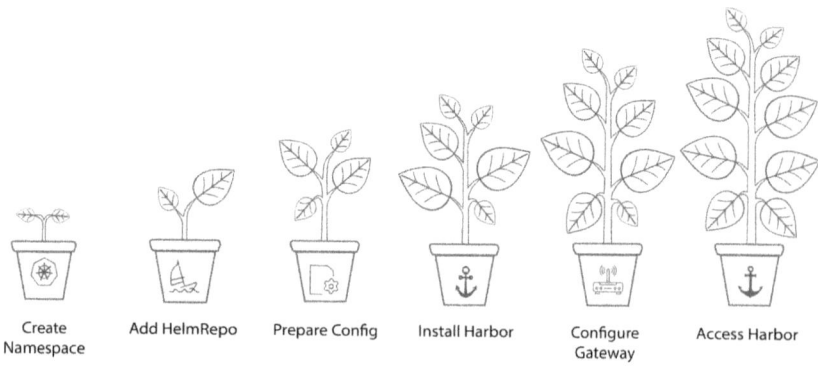

Create Namespace   Add HelmRepo   Prepare Config   Install Harbor   Configure Gateway   Access Harbor

WHAT IS EXECUTIVE BRANDING?

Executive branding is a strategic and intentional process designed to build and manage an executive's reputation, presence, and influence. At its heart, it focuses on identifying and amplifying a leader's unique value proposition (UVP), highlighting their expertise, leadership capabilities, and distinctive professional strengths. Unlike corporate branding, which emphasizes an organization's identity, executive branding is inherently personal. It positions the executive as a representation of the company's vision and values.

Think of executive branding as the art and science of personal storytelling combined with thought, leadership, and deliberate positioning. It involves actively defining and communicating who you are as a leader—your values, voice, and perspective on your industry. When executed effectively, executive branding not only elevates the individual but also strengthens the company's mission and enhances its reputation in the market.

Executive Branding

- Unique Value Proposition
- Expertise
- Leadership Qualities
- Influence

WHY EXECUTIVE BRANDING MATTERS

In today's hyper-connected and transparent business landscape, the importance of a strong executive brand cannot be overstated. As organizations become increasingly interconnected and stakeholders demand authenticity, leaders are now expected to embody their company's values and vision. This heightened visibility places an executive's personal and professional reputation under constant scrutiny—not just from employees and investors, but also from industry peers, potential partners, and the public at large.

A well-crafted executive brand delivers several strategic advantages:

- **Enhanced Credibility and Trust:** Executives with a clear and authentic personal brand exude confidence, earning trust from employees, clients, and investors alike. This trust creates a foundation for respect and solidifies the leader's position as a reliable authority in their field.
- **Career Advancement:** A strong executive brand can accelerate career growth by positioning leaders for promotions, board roles, and high-profile speaking engagements. Being recognized as a trusted industry figure opens doors to new opportunities and enhances professional standing.
- **Increased Influence:** Personal branding enables executives to amplify their voices and broaden their impact. By engaging in thought leadership, they can steer industry discussions, influence emerging trends, and establish themselves as guiding forces within their fields.
- **Alignment with Organizational Success:** When an executive's personal brand aligns seamlessly with the company's mission and values, it becomes a strategic asset. This alignment reinforces the organization's identity, fosters a positive culture, boosts employee morale, and deepens trust across the entire organization.

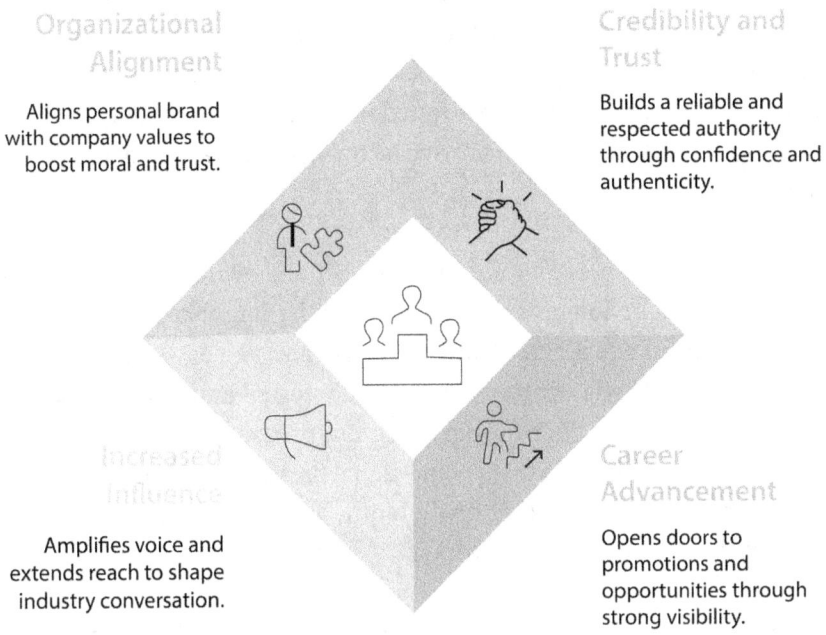

Executive Branding Benefits

Organizational Alignment
Aligns personal brand with company values to boost moral and trust.

Credibility and Trust
Builds a reliable and respected authority through confidence and authenticity.

Increased Influence
Amplifies voice and extends reach to shape industry conversation.

Career Advancement
Opens doors to promotions and opportunities through strong visibility.

Executive branding, then, is more than a personal endeavor—it's a powerful tool that elevates both the individual and the organization they represent.

THE EVOLUTION OF PERSONAL BRANDING

Personal branding is far from a new concept. By the late 20th century, professionals began to recognize the importance of actively managing their reputations to drive career success. Initially, personal branding centered on cultivating trust and credibility within close circles, relying heavily on personal relationships, endorsements, and traditional media to build a reputable presence.

However, the advent of the internet and social media revolutionized personal branding. Platforms like LinkedIn, Twitter, and personal blogs empowered individuals to share insights, engage in global conversations, and connect with audiences far beyond their immediate geographic reach. Personal branding transformed into a dynamic, ongoing process requiring consistent engagement and a strategic approach to maintaining an online presence.

Today, executive branding represents a refined evolution of personal branding. It is no longer solely about visibility but also about earning recognition for a leader's unique expertise and values—qualities that resonate deeply with both internal and external audiences. Modern executive branding goes far beyond an impressive résumé or career milestones; it embodies a compelling digital presence, influential thought leadership, public speaking proficiency, and active participation in community and industry networks.

In its evolved form, executive branding isn't just about who you are—it's about the impact you create, the values you uphold, and the vision you represent.

THE INFLUENCE OF EXECUTIVE BRANDING ON CAREER ADVANCEMENT

The connection between executive branding and career success is well-documented. Leaders who strategically build and manage a strong personal brand are often viewed as innovative, capable, and influential. This perception can provide significant advantages:

- **Accelerated Career Progression:** Executives with a well-defined personal brand are often considered for leadership roles and board positions ahead of their peers. Their heightened visibility ensures they remain top-of-mind for strategic, high-impact opportunities.

- **Expanded Professional Network:** A strong personal brand naturally attracts like-minded professionals, paving the way for valuable connections and collaborations. Building a broad, high-quality network is crucial for fostering innovation, addressing complex challenges, and maintaining a competitive edge.
- **Enhanced Leadership Effectiveness:** Leaders who clearly communicate their personal brand and values tend to inspire and engage their teams more effectively. By consistently aligning their actions with their brand, these executives earn respect and loyalty from employees who value vision and integrity in leadership.

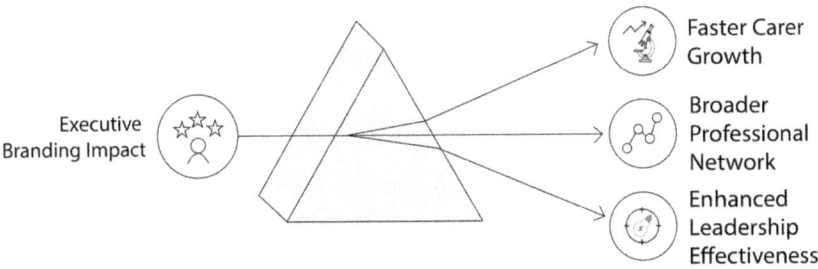

Unvelling The impact of Executing Branding

Executive branding, therefore, isn't just about self-promotion—it's a strategic approach that can unlock faster career growth, deepen professional connections, and improve leadership impact.

HARNESSING THE POWER OF ORGANIZATIONAL INFLUENCE THROUGH A DISTINCT EXECUTIVE BRAND

An executive's brand extends well beyond their personal career achievements; it becomes a reflection of the organization they lead. A thoughtfully crafted executive brand has the power to enhance the company's reputation, attract top-tier talent, and cultivate a unified and vibrant workplace culture. For example, a CEO recognized for their innovative mindset and commitment to inclusivity can inspire these values across the organization. Their personal brand serves as an embodiment of the company's core identity, making it easier to attract and retain employees who align with these principles.

Moreover, executive branding plays a pivotal role in shaping external relationships. In today's landscape—where transparency and trust are indispensable—leaders who effectively articulate their expertise, values, and vision are better equipped to forge meaningful, enduring partnerships. A strong executive brand bolsters credibility with clients and collaborators, reinforces the organization's reputation, and establishes a robust foundation for long-term business success.

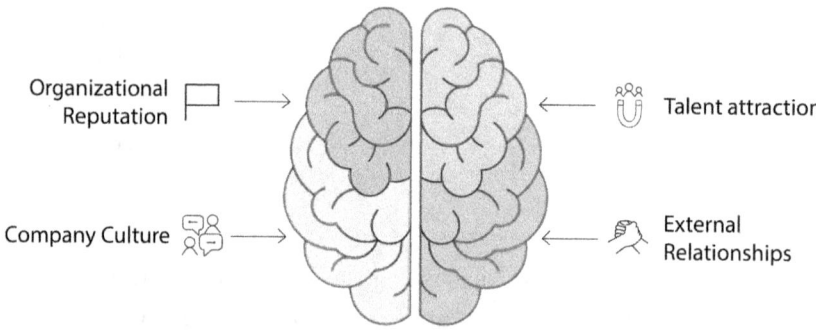

The Impact of Executive Branding

WHY NOW? THE URGENCY OF EXECUTIVE BRANDING IN TODAY'S BUSINESS WORLD

Today's business environment is a fast-paced, dynamic ecosystem where leaders must be visible, agile, and authentically engaged. The COVID-19 pandemic underscored the critical need for leaders who exemplify resilience, empathy, and flexibility—qualities that are vital for navigating uncertainty while maintaining morale and trust. This shift has made it clear that an executive's brand must reflect not only expertise but also emotional intelligence, adaptability, and a steadfast commitment to human-centered leadership.

As digital transformation continues to reshape industries at an unprecedented pace, having a digital-first and adaptable executive brand is no longer optional—it's essential. Leaders who neglect to cultivate a cohesive and compelling brand risk fading into the background, outpaced by those who view branding as a strategic investment. In this ever-evolving landscape, executive branding has transitioned from being a "nice-to-have" to an indispensable element of enduring leadership success.

In summary, executive branding is about more than just career advancement—it encapsulates a leader's identity and influence. This chapter has highlighted the strategic importance of executive branding, showing how it has evolved from a foundational idea into an essential tool for today's leaders. In the chapters that follow, we'll explore how to identify your unique value proposition, crafting a compelling brand story, building a robust digital presence, and ensuring that your executive brand remains authentic, impactful, and future-ready.

UNLOCK THE MAGIC—
SCAN, TO LEARN MORE!

THE COMPONENTS OF EXECUTIVE BRANDING

ESSENTIAL COMPONENTS SUMMARY

Building a powerful executive brand requires more than an impressive résumé or a series of strategic actions; it necessitates the seamless integration of key elements that reflect your professional values and elevate your leadership presence. These foundational components that underpin executive branding: —personal values, professional expertise, visibility, and reputation—are essential for creating a cohesive and impactful executive brand. Together, they shape how colleagues, employees, and the broader industry perceive you.

This chapter offers valuable insights and real-world examples to demonstrate their importance and practical application.

1. PERSONAL VALUES: THE HEART OF YOUR BRAND

At the heart of every strong executive brand lies a clear and compelling set of personal values. These values shape decisions, influence actions, and guide relationships, forming the bedrock of a leader's identity. When clearly defined and consistently communicated, personal values add depth and authenticity to an executive's brand.

The Importance of Personal Values

Aligning a leader's brand with their personal values fosters authenticity and integrity—two qualities that naturally build trust and respect among employees, stakeholders, and peers. Transparent leaders who embody their values create environments that prioritize open communication and ethical behavior, attracting professionals who share similar ideals.

For example, consider a leader whose core value is sustainability. Rather than merely advocating for eco-friendly practices, this leader integrates sustainability into the organization's strategic initiatives. From adopting environmentally responsible policies to championing green innovations, their commitment enhances the brand's credibility. This approach not only appeals to environmentally conscious clients and partners but also attracts like-minded employees, amplifying the brand's influence and impact.

Ultimately, personal values serve as more than guiding principles—they are the foundation of a distinctive executive brand. They resonate deeply with audiences, foster trust and alignment, and drive long-term success.

Maximizing the Power of Personal Values

- **Engage in Self-Reflection:** Identify and articulate your core values by reflecting on your experiences and seeking feedback from colleagues or mentors.
- **Consistent Actions:** Align your daily actions and strategic decisions with your values. Consistency strengthens your brand's authenticity.
- **Communicate Effectively:** Share your values through public speaking, internal communications, and thought leadership pieces, ensuring they are clearly and effectively conveyed.

Personal Values Framework

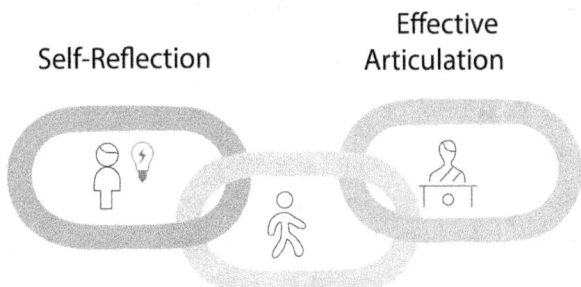

2. DEMONSTRATING YOUR PROFESSIONAL KNOWLEDGE

Your expertise forms the foundation of your executive brand, highlighting your industry insights, depth of knowledge, and unique perspectives. Demonstrating expertise involves showcasing past achievements while also presenting innovative ideas and forward-thinking strategies that shape the future.

The Importance of Professional Expertise

Executives who establish themselves as industry authorities are well-positioned for leadership roles, speaking engagements, and board appointments. Expertise builds credibility, positioning an executive as a trusted leader capable of tackling complex challenges and driving growth.

Take, for example, a CFO with deep knowledge of financial technology trends. By regularly sharing insights on the future of finance—through panel discussions, interviews, or thought leadership articles—this executive can reinforce their status as a leading authority in the field, significantly enhancing their professional reputation and influence.

In essence, showcasing expertise isn't solely about celebrating past successes. It's about consistently offering valuable perspectives that establish you as an indispensable voice in your industry.

Ways to Showcase Your Professional Expertise

- Write Thought Leadership Content: Publish tailored articles, white papers, or blog posts to share your industry knowledge and insights.
- Engage in Public Speaking: Participate in webinars, conferences, and podcasts to reach a broader audience and share your expertise.
- Facilitate Knowledge Sharing: Lead workshops or mentoring sessions within your organization or industry to disseminate knowledge and solidify your reputation as an authority.

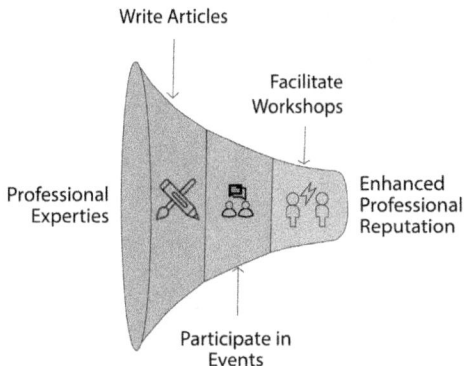

Building Professional Experties Visibility

3. VISIBILITY: MAKING SURE YOUR BRAND STANDS OUT

Visibility breathes life into your executive brand, transforming it from relative obscurity to prominence among the audiences that matter most. It involves strategically participating in initiatives that enhance your presence within the industry and among key influencers. Increased visibility fosters recognition and magnifies the impact of your leadership and insights.

The Importance of Visibility

Visibility builds familiarity—a cornerstone of trust and influence. Executives who actively participate in public forums, industry events, and thought leadership opportunities are perceived as accessible and engaged. This creates a "network effect" that amplifies their influence, enabling their voice to resonate far beyond their immediate connections.

For instance, an executive who regularly shares insights on LinkedIn and speaks at industry panels becomes recognized not only as a subject matter expert but also as an active thought leader. This consistency unlocks new opportunities, such as guest lecturing, media features, and strategic partnerships, further reinforcing their brand and expanding their reach.

Visibility isn't just about being seen; it's about being known for what you stand for and actively shaping your professional landscape.

STRATEGIES TO BOOST YOUR VISIBILITY

In today's digital age, enhancing your visibility as a leader requires strategic, consistent engagement across various platforms and media. By sharing valuable insights, connecting with peers, and participating in key industry events, you can amplify your presence and strengthen your influence. Here are three actionable strategies to help you establish a visible, trusted executive brand:

1. HARNESS THE POWER OF SOCIAL MEDIA

Social media platforms like LinkedIn and Twitter are essential tools for expanding your reach and influence. Start by consistently sharing content that reflects your expertise—whether it's on industry trends, leadership insights, or personal lessons learned. Engaging in conversations by commenting on relevant posts and contributing thoughtful responses shows that you're approachable and invested in your field.

For deeper engagement, consider publishing long-form articles directly on LinkedIn. These pieces allow you to explore critical topics in detail, reinforcing your role as a thought leader while building credibility within your professional community.

2. ENGAGE IN INDUSTRY EVENTS

Attending industry events, both online and in person, is a powerful way to showcase your expertise and build meaningful connections. Participate in conferences, webinars, and networking sessions to expand your professional circle and increase your visibility among industry peers.

To maximize your impact, consider hosting or organizing events yourself. Hosting webinars or moderating discussions positions you as a proactive leader and allows you to engage with audiences on your terms. Speaking at conferences or joining panels further solidifies your authority, attracting new followers who value your insights. Consistent involvement in industry events enhances your reputation and opens doors to future opportunities.

3. COLLABORATE WITH INDUSTRY PEERS

Collaboration is an effective way to extend your reach and connect with new audiences. Partnering with colleagues or respected industry figures to co-author articles, lead webinars, or participate in joint panels broadens your network and strengthens your credibility through association.

Co-authoring content offers readers diverse perspectives while showcasing your ability to collaborate. Similarly, joint webinars and panels enable cross-audience engagement, expanding your influence and demonstrating openness to varied viewpoints. Actively seeking partnerships signals adaptability, dedication to your field, and a collaborative spirit—all vital elements of a respected executive brand.

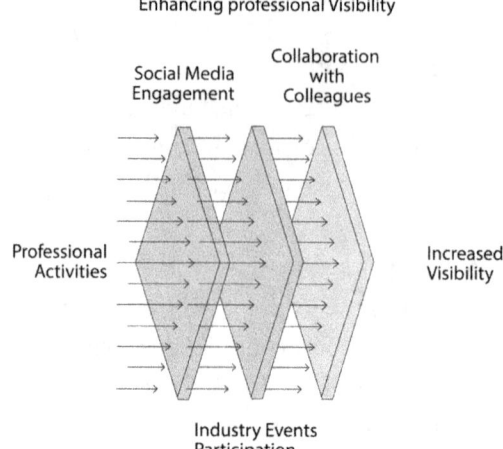

You can significantly increase your visibility by combining these strategies—leveraging social media, engaging in industry events, and collaborating with other leaders. Over time, these efforts will reinforce your executive brand, expand your influence, and position you as a thought leader in your industry.

4. REPUTATION: THE ENDURING IMPACT

Your reputation is the lasting impression shaped at the intersection of your personal values, expertise, and visibility. It reflects how others perceive you—through your actions, decisions, and public presence. A strong reputation is crucial for sustained success, influencing trust, credibility, and the quality of opportunities that come your way.

The Importance of Reputation

A solid reputation opens doors to new opportunities and fosters meaningful, lasting professional connections. Conversely, a tarnished reputation can hinder career advancement and limit prospects, regardless of your skills or achievements. Safeguarding your reputation requires a steadfast commitment to aligning your actions with your stated values and demonstrated expertise.

For instance, a tech CEO renowned for transparent communication and ethical practices will cultivate a reputation that inspires trust, attracting partnerships and top talent. On the other hand, an executive whose reputation is tainted by poor communication or questionable ethics may struggle to maintain influence, no matter their other strengths. Reputation, therefore, isn't just an asset—it's the foundation for enduring success and impactful leadership.

STRATEGIES FOR ESTABLISHING AND SUSTAINING A ROBUST REPUTATION

Establishing and maintaining a strong reputation is vital for leaders, as it paves the way for new opportunities and builds trust and credibility with colleagues, clients, and industry peers. To cultivate a lasting, positive reputation, leaders must act with integrity, approach public engagements thoughtfully, and embrace constructive feedback. Below are three foundational strategies to help you build and sustain a robust reputation.

1. Honor Your Commitments

    Reliability is the cornerstone of a strong reputation. Consistently following through on promises and meeting commitments fosters trust and respect within your professional network. Whether you're leading projects, setting goals, or making decisions, ensure your actions align with your commitments. Even when circumstances don't go as planned, taking responsibility and demonstrating accountability underscores your integrity. By being someone others can depend on, you reinforce your reputation as a trustworthy and professional leader.

2. Engage Thoughtfully

   How you manage public interactions and navigate challenges significantly shapes your reputation. Approach every engagement—whether it's a public speaking event, media interview, or social media response—with care, honesty, and poise. When addressing feedback, especially criticism, respond with transparency and a willingness to consider different perspectives. Handling setbacks or critical moments with calmness and consistency demonstrates maturity and reinforces your values. Leaders who navigate public engagements authentically and thoughtfully are more likely to earn credibility and trust.

3. Seek Feedback and Reflect Regularly

   Sustaining a strong reputation requires self-reflection and a commitment to continuous improvement. Actively seek feedback from trusted colleagues, team members, and advisors to gain insights into how your actions are perceived. Constructive input allows you to recognize both strengths and areas for growth, enabling you to make adjustments that strengthen your reputation. Engaging with feedback demonstrates humility and a commitment to personal development, enhancing your image as a leader who values growth and excellence.

   In essence, a strong reputation is built on consistency, thoughtful engagement, and a willingness to evolve. By following these strategies, you can cultivate a reputation that not only reflects your values and expertise but also endures over time.

By honoring your commitments, handling public interactions with care, and seeking regular feedback, you'll create a reputation that is both resilient and respected. Over time, these actions will not only enhance your professional image but also establish you as a leader who exemplifies integrity, accountability, and a dedication to growth.

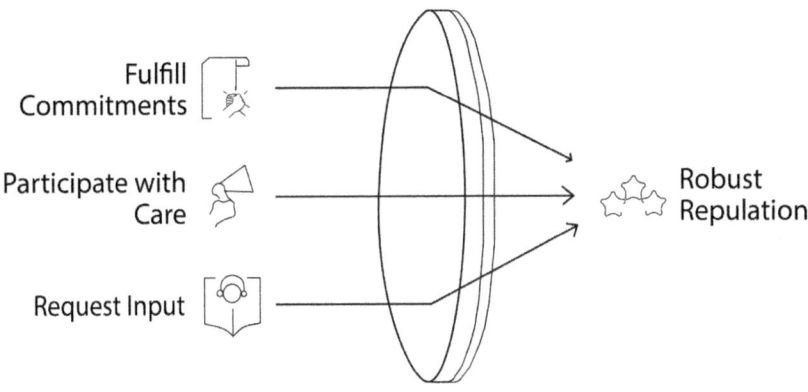

UNIFYING EVERYTHING

Executive branding is built on four key elements: personal values, expertise, visibility, and reputation. Personal values serve as the foundation for authentic leadership, while expertise establishes your authority. Visibility ensures your brand reaches the right audience, and reputation solidifies your leadership's lasting impact.

When aligned and supported by consistent actions and strategic messaging, these components create a cohesive brand that drives career growth, amplifies leadership influence, and fosters organizational success. Throughout this guide, we will explore how to define your unique value, craft a compelling narrative, and implement strategies for brand growth and sustainability.

Mastering these elements is essential for executives aiming to thrive in today's competitive landscape, advancing both their careers and organizational impact.

UNLOCK THE MAGIC—
SCAN, TO LEARN MORE!

IDENTIFYING YOUR UNIQUE VALUE PROPOSITION

AN INSIGHT INTO SELF-ASSESSMENT TOOLS

In the competitive world of business leadership, an executive's unique value proposition (UVP) is the key element that sets them apart from their peers. This proposition is more than just a statement—it's a powerful declaration of the specific skills, strengths, and experiences that make you uniquely valuable to your industry and organization. This chapter introduces practical exercises designed to help you identify your UVP and demonstrates how aligning it with both personal and organizational goals can elevate your career trajectory and amplify your leadership influence.

UNDERSTANDING THE UNIQUE VALUE PROPOSITION

An executive's UVP is not just a tagline; it is a strategic statement that encapsulates your core competencies, differentiating qualities, and the unique value you provide to your organization and stakeholders. Your UVP serves as the cornerstone of your personal brand, guiding your communication and ensuring consistency. It enables you to clearly articulate what makes you stand out to colleagues, team members, board members, and industry leaders.

IDENTIFYING YOUR UVP: SELF-ASSESSMENT TOOLS AND TECHNIQUES

To pinpoint your UVP, you must have a deep understanding of your strengths, values, and the specific qualities you bring to your leadership role. Self-assessment tools can provide invaluable insights, offering an objective perspective on how your skills and attributes align with the demands of your role and the needs of your organization. Here are several practical tools to help you identify your UVP:

1. SWOT Analysis (Strengths, Weaknesses, Opportunities, Threats): A SWOT analysis tailored to your personal and professional life offers a structured perspective on where you excel, areas for improvement, opportunities for growth, and potential risks. Reflect on your strengths and how they uniquely position you in your field, and identify areas for development.
2. 360-Degree Feedback: Gathering feedback from peers, subordinates, mentors, and superiors provides a multi-dimensional view of how others perceive your strengths and contributions. This feedback can reveal attributes that may be invisible to you but invaluable to others, helping you refine your UVP.
3. Personality and Leadership Style Assessments: Tools such as the Myers-Briggs Type Indicator (MBTI), DiSC, or CliftonStrengths provide insights into your natural inclinations, interpersonal style, and leadership approach. Understanding your personality traits and how they translate into leadership behaviors will help you craft a UVP that is both authentic and impactful.
4. Skill and Competency Evaluation: Review your past projects and achievements to assess your technical, strategic, and interpersonal skills. Identify the core competencies that consistently drive your success, enabling you to highlight the unique blend of skills that set you apart.

Values Clarification Exercises: Reflect on the principles that guide your decisions and actions. Leaders who articulate their values and act consistently with them establish credibility and trust within their organizations, making values alignment a powerful differentiator.

ALIGNING YOUR UVP WITH ORGANIZATIONAL GOALS

Once you've identified your UVP, the next step is to ensure it aligns with your organization's goals and mission. This alignment amplifies your impact by positioning you as a leader who not only brings unique strengths to the table but also actively contributes to the organization's strategic objectives. Here's how to achieve this alignment:

- **Map Your UVP to Key Business Objectives:** Consider the organization's priorities—whether innovation, growth, operational efficiency, or customer satisfaction—and identify where your strengths can have the greatest influence. By linking your UVP to these objectives, you create a compelling narrative about how your unique abilities support the company's vision.
- **Communicate with Intention:** Your UVP should inform how you present yourself in meetings, strategic discussions, and team interactions. By consistently demonstrating how your strengths support organizational goals, you reinforce your unique value and strengthen your brand.
- **Evolve with Organizational Needs:** As your organization grows or pivots, so too should your UVP. Periodically re-evaluate your UVP to ensure it reflects both your evolving expertise and the organization's current needs, ensuring your brand remains aligned and relevant.

By mastering your UVP, you gain the clarity and confidence to differentiate yourself and demonstrate the distinct value you bring. In the following sections, we will explore how to incorporate your UVP into your executive brand narrative and communicate it effectively to maximize your career impact and influence.

YOUR UNIQUE VALUE PROPOSITION MUST ADDRESS ESSENTIAL QUESTIONS:

- What unique strengths and expertise do I offer?
- In what ways do these strengths address key challenges or enhance the value of my organization and industry?
- What sets me apart as a leader, making collaboration or following me a compelling choice?

Unique value proposition

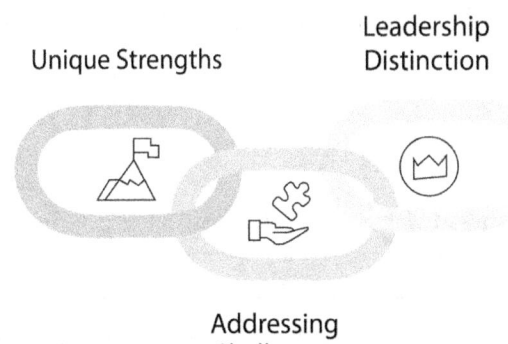

Unique Strengths

Leadership Distinction

Addressing Challenges

A THOUGHTFULLY DESIGNED UNIQUE VALUE PROPOSITION

A well-crafted unique value proposition (UVP) not only reflects your core values but also aligns with the goals of the organization you represent. This alignment creates a compelling narrative that enhances your professional presence and strengthens your leadership identity.

WHY ALIGNING YOUR UNIQUE VALUE PROPOSITION WITH YOUR GOALS MATTERS

To be truly effective, your UVP must be embedded within a larger framework that connects your personal strengths and aspirations to both your career goals and your organization's strategic objectives. When your unique capabilities resonate with the company's mission, you become more than just a leader; you become an indispensable catalyst for success.

Consider a leader in a technology firm whose defining traits are creativity and a forward-thinking approach to strategy. Their UVP might focus on driving innovative digital transformation. When this aligns seamlessly with the organization's goal of leading in technological advancement, the executive's brand evolves into a powerful asset that accelerates the company's growth and mission.

Structured Activities for Personal Evaluation

1. Identifying your unique value proposition requires a structured, reflective self-assessment. The following exercises are designed to help you uncover your core strengths, distinguish what sets you apart, and craft a UVP that aligns with both your career aspirations and organizational goals.
2. Values and Vision Alignment Exercise: Reflect on your personal values and how they align with your organization's mission. List your top five values and analyze how each one supports your role and contributes to the company's goals. This exercise strengthens self-awareness and solidifies your commitment to aligning personal and organizational priorities.
3. Defining Your Key Strengths: List your top skills and abilities, particularly those that have contributed to your success in leadership roles. Identify specific examples where these strengths have made a significant impact, either in past roles or

current projects. This exercise provides clarity on the qualities that should be central to your UVP.
4. Future Goals Mapping: Define your career aspirations and the impact you wish to achieve within your organization. Consider how your unique strengths can support both your professional growth and the company's strategic direction. This exercise ensures your UVP is grounded in your current role while remaining forward-looking.
5. Competitor and Peer Comparison: Identify peers or competitors in your industry known for their leadership qualities. Assess what differentiates them and consider what sets you apart. This perspective offers valuable insights into your unique positioning and competitive edge.
6. Crafting Your UVP Statement: Using the insights from these exercises, draft a UVP statement that succinctly captures your distinct value. This statement should encapsulate your strengths, values, and alignment with organizational objectives, resonating with both internal and external stakeholders.

By thoroughly engaging in these structured activities, you will craft a UVP that not only highlights your unique strengths but also aligns with your organization's goals, positioning you as a leader with both clarity and purpose. In the following chapters, we'll explore how to integrate this UVP into your executive brand narrative, ensuring your message is authentic, impactful, and aligned with your long-term leadership vision.

ACTIVITY 1: CONSIDER YOUR ABILITIES AND TALENTS

- **Highlight Your Key Strengths:** List all the skills where you excel, including both technical abilities and interpersonal strengths. These might include expertise in financial analysis, strategic planning, effective communication, and strong team leadership.
- **Discover Your Distinct Advantages:** Identify the skills that differentiate you from others in similar positions. These unique qualities, such as the ability to innovate under pressure or foster collaboration across diverse teams, are what set you apart.
- **Collect Insights:** Gather feedback from colleagues, mentors, and direct reports to understand your strengths from an external perspective. Their insights may reveal strengths you've overlooked or validate those you've already recognized.

Outcome: By the end of this exercise, you will have a clear list of your most powerful and distinctive qualities.

TASK 2: IDENTIFY YOUR MAJOR ACCOMPLISHMENTS

- **Showcase Your Key Achievements:** Detail significant milestones in your career that showcase your strengths in action. Whenever possible, include measurable outcomes, such as "Spearheaded a team that increased revenue by 25%" or "Implemented a cost-reduction strategy that saved $1 million annually."
- **Link Accomplishments to Abilities:** Identify the strengths and skills that contributed to each of your accomplishments.
- **Recognize Trends:** Look for patterns among your successes. Are you consistently pushing the boundaries of innovation or driving impactful initiatives? These patterns reveal your core value as a leader.

Outcome: This exercise will both highlight your strengths and demonstrate how you've effectively applied them in impactful ways.

Identifying and showcasing major accomplishments

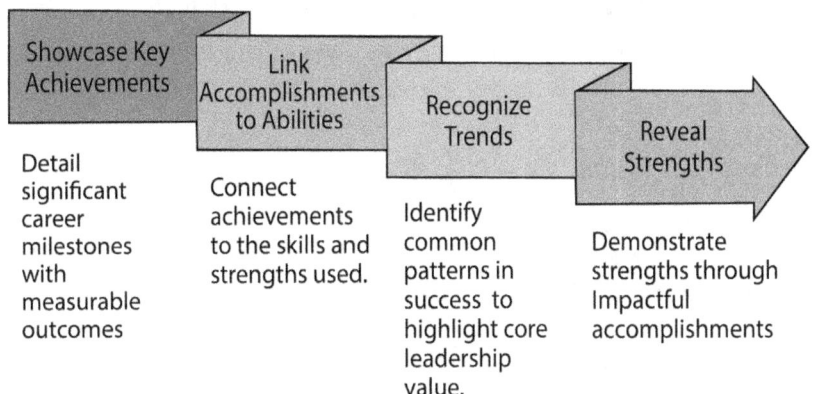

EXERCISE 3: EVALUATE YOUR INDUSTRY AND ORGANIZATIONAL REQUIREMENTS

Examine Your Sector:

Explore the latest trends and challenges within your industry. Identify the key obstacles and the skills most in demand. What are the critical hurdles your sector faces, and which competencies are becoming indispensable?

Assess Your Organization's Strategic Objectives:

Clarify your company's strategic goals and determine the key attributes it seeks in its leaders. For instance, if your organization plans to expand into new markets, expertise in global strategy and cross-cultural communication will be essential.

ALIGN YOUR STRENGTHS WITH INDUSTRY DEMANDS:

Identify how your unique strengths and experiences align with the gaps or opportunities in your industry and organization.

The Result:

Understanding how your abilities correspond with both industry demands and organizational goals is fundamental to crafting a distinctive value proposition that resonates and creates a meaningful impact.

Creating Your Distinct Value Proposition

After completing your self-assessment exercises, use the following formula to craft your unique value proposition:

"I am a professional with a strong foundation in [core strengths/skills]. I have achieved notable milestones that demonstrate these strengths. I deliver value by [explaining how these strengths align with organizational or industry needs]."

Example:

"I am a dynamic tech executive specializing in digital transformation and strategic innovation, driving forward-thinking solutions. I have successfully led teams to develop AI-driven initiatives, resulting in a 30% increase in productivity and a $2 million reduction in operational costs. My ability to anticipate technology trends and manage complex projects aligns seamlessly with the industry's focus on automation and efficiency, positioning me as a key asset for organizations pursuing digital excellence."

Harmonizing Your Unique Value Proposition with
Professional and Organizational Objectives

Creating your unique value proposition is only the first step. To maximize its impact, it must be integrated into your professional strategy and daily interactions. Here's how:

1. Internal Communication

   Incorporate your unique value proposition into all interactions with your team and stakeholders. Use it as the foundation for discussions around new projects, strategic initiatives, and innovative solutions.

2. Public Presence

   Embed your unique value proposition into your public-facing materials, such as your LinkedIn profile, professional bio, and speaking topics at conferences. This approach enhances your personal brand and ensures that your strengths and contributions are visible to colleagues, clients, and peers.

CAREER ADVANCEMENT

Align your unique value proposition with your ongoing professional development. As you acquire new skills and gain experience, refine your value proposition to reflect your evolving strengths and contributions.

Integrating Your Unique Value Proposition

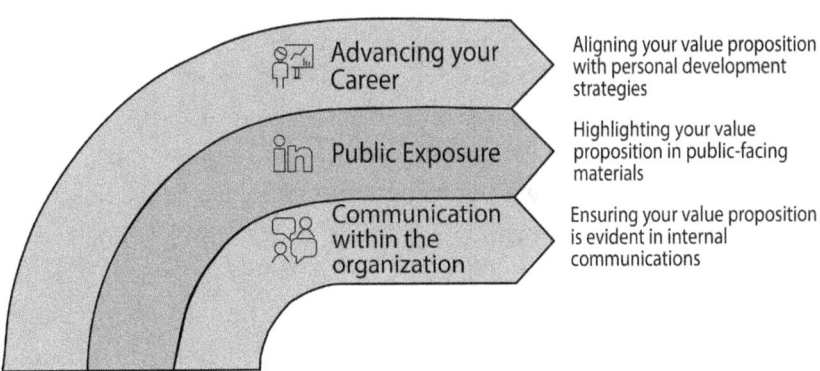

OPTIMIZING YOUR UNIQUE VALUE PROPOSITION

To ensure your unique value proposition aligns optimally, emphasize your strengths in sustainability and innovation. Connect these strengths to your organization's initiatives that prioritize eco-friendly practices or advancements in sustainable technology. Position yourself as a leading authority in these areas, reinforcing your brand with a steadfast commitment to these principles.

CONTINUOUSLY ENHANCING YOUR UNIQUE VALUE PROPOSITION

Your professional journey evolves as dynamically as the business landscape. To stay relevant, your unique value proposition must be adaptable, growing alongside your experiences and the changing demands of your industry. Regularly revisiting and refining your value proposition ensures it aligns with your career goals and industry shifts.

REGULAR ASSESSMENTS:

Schedule biannual or annual evaluations of your unique value proposition. During these reviews, reflect on your achievements, gather feedback, and implement necessary updates to accurately represent recent successes and career advancements.

In conclusion, recognizing and articulating your unique value proposition is vital to building a strong and influential executive brand. By identifying your core strengths, aligning them with organizational needs, and communicating them effectively, you position yourself as a leader primed for driving growth and innovation. The next chapter explores crafting a compelling executive brand narrative that connects with your audience and enhances your leadership identity.

IN-DEPTH QUESTIONS TO HELP EXECUTIVES DEFINE THEIR UVP

1. Self-Reflection on Core Strengths and Skills

Self-reflection is essential for uncovering the unique qualities that define you as a leader. It helps identify strengths that not only come naturally but also deliver meaningful impact. The following introspective questions can guide this process:

- What tasks or projects come naturally to me, and where have I consistently excelled?
- Reflect on activities where you thrive, experience a sense of flow, and produce exceptional results. These areas, whether in problem-solving, strategic planning, or team leadership, highlight your natural strengths and areas of significant value.
- What feedback do I frequently receive from peers, direct reports, or mentors?
- Analyze recurring themes in the feedback from those who work closely with you. Whether recognized for analytical thinking, effective communication, or empathy, this input provides a mirror to your strengths and informs the reputation you can build.
- What do I enjoy most about my role, and how does this align with my strengths?
- Consider the tasks you find most fulfilling and why. These often align with your strengths, revealing areas where you are both effective and passionate. For example, a love for mentoring could indicate strong leadership and communication skills.
- Which of my skills or qualities have had the most measurable impact in my career?
- Reflect on skills that have driven measurable outcomes—whether through cost savings, innovation, or improved team performance. Identifying these impactful strengths clarifies your core contributions and highlights areas for brand emphasis.

- If I were to mentor someone, what unique skills or approaches would I teach?
- Imagine yourself mentoring others. The skills or methods you feel confident teaching reflect your unique strengths. These insights can guide how you position your leadership capabilities.

By engaging with these questions, you can identify and articulate the strengths that distinguish your leadership style. Leveraging these insights allows you to enhance your brand, focus on impactful areas, and deliver greater value in your career.

2. Identifying Differentiators

Defining what sets you apart is crucial in a competitive landscape. Your differentiators extend beyond basic skills to include unique attributes, perspectives, and approaches that make your leadership style memorable. These guiding questions can help uncover your personal differentiators:

- What do I offer that few others in my industry or company do?
- Identify the skills, insights, or capabilities that make you stand out—such as a combination of technical expertise and interpersonal skills, or a talent for identifying overlooked growth opportunities. Highlighting these traits reinforces your unique value to your team and industry.
- How would my direct reports or colleagues describe my leadership style?
- Consider feedback from those who work closely with you. Whether you're known for empathetic leadership or decisive decision-making, understanding these perceptions helps articulate your unique approach.
- What experiences or perspectives do I bring from outside my industry that give me an edge?
- Reflect on cross-industry insights or unconventional experiences that differentiate you. For example, transitioning from finance to

technology might give you a data-driven perspective that's rare in your field. Recognizing and leveraging these insights can strengthen your leadership brand.

By identifying and emphasizing these unique elements, you can build a reputation that reflects your individuality, strengthens your brand, and positions you as a standout leader in your field.

- In what ways do I approach problem-solving differently, and what results has this produced?
- Analyze your unique problem-solving strategies, such as viewing challenges from multiple angles or fostering collaboration. Highlight the results of these methods, such as improved processes or innovative solutions.
- Which of my qualities have been most frequently praised by clients, stakeholders, or peers?
- Consistently acknowledged qualities, like adaptability or creativity, provide valuable insights into your differentiators and strengthen your reputation.

By embracing these unique traits, you cultivate a distinct brand that reflects originality, strength, and value. These qualities not only define your leadership style but also position you as a memorable and impactful leader.

3. Contribution to Organizational Goals

Aligning your strengths with your organization's strategic goals ensures that your unique value proposition (UVP) is not only distinct but also deeply relevant to the company's mission. By understanding how your skills and perspectives contribute to your organization's success, you can position yourself as a pivotal leader focused on delivering impactful results where they matter most. The following questions are designed to help you evaluate how your abilities and leadership style align with your organization's objectives and address its key challenges.

- What Are the Current Strategic Goals or Priorities of My Organization, and How Do My Skills Directly Support or Advance These Goals?
- Start by identifying your organization's primary objectives—whether they center on growth, innovation, market expansion, or operational efficiency. Then, assess how your specific skills and expertise contribute to these aims. For example, if the company is prioritizing digital transformation, your technical expertise and experience with change management could be critical assets. Aligning your strengths with organizational goals not only enhances your relevance but also demonstrates your commitment to the company's mission.
- What Unique Perspectives or Skills Can I Bring to Help My Organization Navigate Current Industry Challenges or Trends?
- Every industry faces unique challenges and evolving trends. Your ability to address these effectively can add significant value. Consider any specialized knowledge, cross-functional expertise, or innovative thinking you bring to the table. For instance, you might help the organization tackle issues such as technological disruption, regulatory changes, or shifting consumer behaviors. By aligning your insights with industry trends, you position yourself as a forward-thinking leader capable of steering the organization through complex challenges.
- How Have I Directly Contributed to My Company's Success or Growth in Recent Years? What Results Have I Achieved That Would Have Been Difficult Without My Specific Expertise?
- Reflect on the measurable ways you've contributed to your organization's achievements. This could include leading key projects, optimizing critical processes, or helping the company reach significant goals. Be specific about your impact—for example, spearheading a cost-saving initiative that boosted profitability or leading a team to successfully launch a new product line. Showcasing these achievements highlights your unique expertise and reinforces your value as someone who delivers measurable success.

- What Problems Do I Solve Exceptionally Well Within My Company, and What Is the Direct Value of Solving These Problems?
- Identify the challenges you are consistently relied upon to address. Are you the go-to person for crisis management, strategic planning, or team motivation? Consider the tangible value of solving these problems—whether it's driving efficiency, improving team cohesion, or enhancing customer satisfaction. By clarifying the problems you excel at resolving, you solidify your role as a vital contributor to organizational stability and growth.
- How Does My Leadership Style Enhance the Culture, Productivity, or Morale of My Organization?
- Your leadership style plays a significant role in shaping your organization's culture and environment. Reflect on how your approach—whether it's collaborative, transparent, innovative, or supportive—positively influences productivity and morale. For example, if you prioritize empowering your team, consider how this has fostered creativity, improved performance, or strengthened employee loyalty. Articulating these contributions emphasizes your role in creating a workplace culture where people thrive and achieve shared goals.

By aligning your strengths with your organization's needs, you establish a UVP that is not only unique but also essential to the company's success. This alignment underscores your investment in the organization's future and highlights your ability to provide direct, measurable value. In doing so, your personal brand becomes synonymous with progress, problem-solving, and a steadfast commitment to advancing the company's strategic vision.

4. Personal and Professional Values

   Your values form the foundation of your leadership style, guiding how you make decisions, interact with others, and navigate challenges. They are integral to your unique value proposition (UVP), as they reflect your character and commitment to ethical leadership. By clarifying your values, you not only enhance your self-awareness but also convey a clear and authentic message to those around you. Reflecting on the following questions can help you better understand how your values influence your leadership approach, strengthen your relationships, and align with your organization's mission.

- What Values Do I Hold That Guide My Leadership Decisions and Actions?
- Consider the principles that influence your choices and behaviors as a leader. Core values such as integrity, resilience, empathy, or accountability can shape everything from strategic planning to daily interactions. Identifying these guiding values provides a solid foundation for consistent, values-driven leadership. For instance, if integrity is central to your approach, you may prioritize honesty and transparency, creating a leadership style that earns respect and trust.
- What Issues or Causes Am I Most Passionate About in My Industry, and How Does This Passion Shape My Role?
- Think about the issues within your industry that resonate deeply with you—such as diversity and inclusion, innovation, sustainability, or ethical business practices. Passion for a particular cause often shapes how you approach your role and the priorities you set. For example, a leader passionate about sustainability might champion environmentally friendly initiatives, aligning their work with a broader purpose. Recognizing these passions allows you to position yourself as a purpose-driven leader committed to creating a meaningful impact in your field.
- How Do I Prioritize and Demonstrate Core Values Like Integrity and Transparency in Daily Interactions?
- Values like integrity and transparency are not just high-level concepts—they are reflected in everyday actions and interactions. Consider how you embody these values in your communication style, feedback approach, and team relationships. Leaders who

prioritize transparency may openly share information, acknowledge mistakes, and foster an atmosphere of trust. By consistently demonstrating these values, you create an environment of openness and dependability, enhancing your influence and credibility.

- What Qualities Do I Embody That Inspire Trust and Loyalty Among My Team Members and Peers?
- Trust and loyalty are cultivated through consistent actions aligned with your values. Reflect on the qualities others frequently recognize in you—such as dependability, fairness, empathy, or accountability. These traits are key to building strong and lasting relationships with your team and colleagues. For instance, a leader known for fairness may foster a culture of inclusivity and respect, strengthening team loyalty. Understanding which qualities inspire trust helps you intentionally cultivate them, deepening connections and improving team morale.
- How Do My Values Align With My Organization's, and How Does This Alignment Strengthen My Leadership Impact?
- When your personal values align with your organization's principles, it creates a powerful synergy that amplifies your leadership impact. Consider how values like innovation, integrity, or social responsibility resonate with your company's mission. This alignment enhances credibility and allows you to lead initiatives that highlight shared priorities. For example, if both you and your organization prioritize community involvement, you can spearhead programs that reflect this mutual commitment, reinforcing a unified vision. This alignment not only strengthens your personal brand but also establishes you as an authentic leader dedicated to advancing organizational goals.

By understanding and articulating your values, you lead with clarity and purpose. Embedding these values into your UVP creates a leadership identity that is authentic, trusted, and aligned with a greater mission. When your actions consistently reflect your principles, you establish yourself as a leader who stands for something meaningful—making a lasting impact both within and beyond your organization.

5. Identifying Your Ideal Audience

    Crafting a well-defined unique value proposition (UVP) goes beyond highlighting your strengths and values—it requires a deep understanding of the people you aim to influence and impact. Whether your audience consists of stakeholders, employees, industry peers, or the general public, knowing who they are enables you to tailor your brand to resonate with those who matter most to your mission. Reflecting on the following questions will help you define your ideal audience and create a UVP that is relevant, impactful, and effective.

- Who Do I Most Want to Influence or Impact with My Work?
- Begin by identifying the specific groups or individuals you aim to reach and inspire. These could include your team members, senior stakeholders, industry leaders, clients, or the public at large. Understanding your target audience allows you to address their unique needs, challenges, and interests.
- For instance, if employees are your primary audience, your UVP might emphasize qualities such as empathy, transparency, and empowerment. Defining your audience enables you to craft a message that resonates most strongly with those you wish to lead and influence.
- What Does My Ideal Audience Expect from a Leader in My Position, and How Can I Meet or Exceed Those Expectations?
- Every audience has expectations of leaders based on their role, industry, and organizational culture. Take time to reflect on what your audience values most in a leader—whether it's decisiveness, innovation, integrity, or collaboration. By understanding these expectations, you can adapt your leadership approach to not only meet but exceed them, strengthening your reputation.

- For example, if industry peers expect you to be forward-thinking, demonstrating your expertise in emerging trends or innovations can deepen your connection with them and solidify your standing as a visionary leader.
- How Do I Wish to Be Perceived by My Peers, My Team, and My Industry at Large?
- Consider the qualities and reputation you want to cultivate in the eyes of your various audiences, including direct reports, colleagues, and the broader industry. Do you aspire to be seen as an empathetic leader who prioritizes team well-being? A strategic visionary driving innovation? Or a reliable expert in your field?
- By defining how you wish to be perceived, you can make intentional choices in your actions, communication, and presence. This deliberate effort ensures that your image aligns with your leadership goals and resonates with your ideal audience.
- What Unique Value Do I Bring That Resonates Most Strongly with This Audience, and Why?
- Identify the specific strengths, skills, or perspectives that make you uniquely valuable to your audience. These might include your problem-solving approach, dedication to social impact, or commitment to mentoring. Think about why these qualities resonate with your audience and how they address their needs or challenges.
- For example, if clients value ethical leadership, emphasizing your dedication to transparency and fairness can build trust. Understanding what resonates most with your audience allows you to center your brand on qualities that they find meaningful and relevant.
- If I Were to Receive a Public Endorsement from a Respected Peer or Mentor, What Qualities or Achievements Would I Want Them to Highlight?
- Imagine receiving a public endorsement from someone you respect—a peer, mentor, or industry leader. What aspects of your leadership or accomplishments would you want them to spotlight?

Whether it's your ability to inspire, your strategic insight, or your resilience, this exercise helps you identify the traits and achievements you value most.

These insights guide you in nurturing and showcasing the aspects of your brand that you want your audience to associate with you.

By understanding your ideal audience and their expectations, you can craft a UVP that speaks directly to the people you most want to influence. Aligning your UVP with your audience's needs not only enhances its relevance but also helps you build a leadership brand that resonates deeply and authentically. This alignment strengthens your impact, allowing you to connect meaningfully with your community and establish a lasting reputation as a leader who truly understands and supports those around them.

6. Defining Your Long-Term Vision and Impact

A powerful unique value proposition (UVP) goes beyond your current strengths and values; it is also a reflection of your long-term goals and the legacy you aim to create. Defining your vision and desired impact helps you align daily actions with the greater purpose you hope to achieve, guiding you toward meaningful and lasting contributions. The following questions will help you connect your UVP to your long-term aspirations, ensuring that your leadership journey reflects not only who you are but also the legacy you wish to leave.

- What Is My Long-Term Vision for My Career, and How Does My Current Role or Expertise Support This Vision?

Begin by envisioning where you want your career to lead in the coming years. Are you focused on rising to a higher leadership position, driving innovation within your industry, or mentoring the next generation of leaders? Understanding your long-term career vision allows you to see how your current role and skills are contributing to that path. For instance, if your goal is to lead an organization through a major transformation, reflect on how your expertise in change management or strategic planning is already supporting this journey. A clear vision serves as a compass, guiding your growth and aligning your current efforts with your future aspirations.

- What Impact Do I Hope to Have on My Industry, Organization, or Community?

Think about the broader impact you want your work to have—not just for yourself, but for the industry, organization, or community you serve. This could involve leading advancements in technology, championing ethical business practices, or creating opportunities for underrepresented groups. Defining the change you wish to drive shapes your UVP and positions you as a leader with a purpose beyond personal success. For example, if your goal is to make your industry more sustainable, you can prioritize this focus in your leadership approach by advocating for policies and practices that align with sustainability goals.

- How Do I Want to Be Remembered by Those Who Work With or Learn From Me?

Reflect on the impression you want to leave on those around you—whether they are colleagues, mentees, clients, or team members. Do you aspire to be remembered as a supportive mentor, a bold innovator, or a compassionate leader? Defining how you wish to be remembered clarifies the qualities you value most and ensures that you actively embody these traits. This perspective on legacy serves as a guiding framework, inspiring you to act in ways that reinforce the positive impact you hope to have on others.

- What Do I Consider to Be My Greatest Professional Purpose, and How Does This Purpose Guide My Daily Actions and Decisions?

Your professional purpose is the driving force behind your career. It motivates you, defines your passion, and shapes your decisions. Reflect on what gives your work meaning—whether it's creating value for others, advancing knowledge, or inspiring positive change. By identifying this purpose, you can intentionally align your actions to support it. For example, if your purpose is to empower your team, you might prioritize transparency, create opportunities for growth, and encourage open communication. This alignment ensures that your career remains consistently fulfilling and impactful.

- What Is the Lasting Contribution I Hope to Make Within My Industry or Organization, and What Makes Me Uniquely Suited to Make This Contribution?

Consider the specific contribution you want to leave as a legacy in your field or organization. This might involve solving a persistent problem, introducing an innovative approach to a traditional process, or fostering a culture of inclusivity and integrity. Reflect on what makes you uniquely suited to achieve this contribution, such as your distinctive experiences, skills, or perspectives. For instance, if you are passionate about driving change in healthcare, your combined expertise in technology and patient advocacy might position you to deliver transformative solutions. Recognizing your unique role in making a lasting impact adds depth to your UVP, portraying you as a purpose-driven leader prepared to make a meaningful difference.

By defining your long-term vision and desired impact, you craft a UVP that not only highlights your strengths but also resonates with a larger purpose. This alignment of goals, actions, and aspirations allows you to lead with intention, inspiring those around you and creating a legacy that extends beyond your immediate achievements. A UVP built on a clear, purpose-driven vision not only defines your present identity as a leader but also lays the foundation for a lasting impact that embodies your highest ideals and ambitions.

ADDITIONAL EXERCISES TO FURTHER REFINE YOUR UVP

1. Peer Interview Exercise

   Reach out to trusted colleagues, mentors, or even former clients and ask them what they believe sets you apart. Frame your question to elicit specific examples of how your presence or input made a meaningful difference. Their feedback may uncover unique strengths you tend to overlook or take for granted.

2. Analyze High-Impact Projects

   Reflect on past projects where you played a pivotal role and analyze the factors behind your success. What did you do differently compared to others? How did your approach reflect your values and leverage your strengths? Identifying these patterns can highlight consistent qualities that form the foundation of your UVP.

3. Future-Focused Visualization

   Picture yourself five years into the future. What role are you playing, and what strengths have helped you achieve this position? How do you envision others describing your journey and contributions? This exercise can help you pinpoint the skills and qualities that will continue to drive your growth and impact.

4. UVP Worksheet

Develop a worksheet to clearly articulate the following components of your UVP:

- Top 3 Skills and Strengths: Summarize the key skills that best align with your UVP.
- Key Accomplishments: List three accomplishments that showcase your strengths in action.
- Core Values: Define three values that guide your decisions and actions.
- Long-Term Goal: Identify your primary long-term career objective.
- Audience Impact: Write a concise statement about who you want to impact and how you intend to do so.

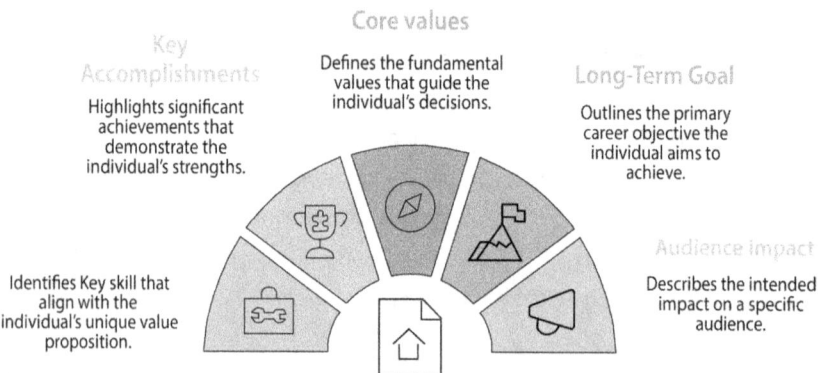

Personal Development Worksheet

Use this worksheet to summarize your UVP in a concise statement. This format can help you quickly refer to your UVP as you build your brand narrative.

BRINGING IT ALL TOGETHER: CRAFTING YOUR UVP STATEMENT

Refine your unique value proposition (UVP) into a concise statement highlighting your strengths, achievements, and impact. Use the formula: "I am a [role/expert] known for [core strengths]. I bring value through [key achievements] and aim to [goal or audience impact].

Example:

"I am a technology leader known for strategic foresight and ethical innovation, increasing productivity by 35% and advancing sustainability. This chapter offers prompts to help executives craft UVPs that resonate with audiences and align with leadership goals."

UVP WORKSHEET

1. TOP 3 SKILLS AND STRENGTHS

- **Instructions** : Identify and summarize the most impactful skills or strengths that set you apart. Consider both technical and soft skills.

- **Skill/Strength #1:** _____

  Why is this skill/strength valuable?
  _____

- **Skill/Strength #2:** _____

  How does this skill/strength differentiate you?
  _____

- **Skill/Strength #3:** _____

    How has this skill/strength impacted your work or organization?
    _____

2. KEY ACCOMPLISHMENTS

- **Instructions**: List three accomplishments that best illustrate your expertise and unique approach. Provide context and results where possible.

- **Accomplishment #1:** _____

    Describe the context and result:
    _____

- **Accomplishment #2:** _____

    Describe the context and result:
    _____

- **Accomplishment #3:** _____

    Describe the context and result:
    _____

3. CORE VALUES

- **Instructions**: Define three core values that guide your decisions, interactions, and leadership style.

- **Value #1:** _____

    How does this value influence your leadership?
    _____

- **Value #2:** _____

    Why is this value important to you and your team?
    _____

- **Value #3:** _____

    How does this value align with your organization's goals?
    _____

4. LONG-TERM GOAL

- **Instructions** : Identify your primary long-term career goal. Consider how this goal connects with your skills, values, and professional aspirations.

- **Goal Statement:** My long-term career goal is to
_____

Why is this goal meaningful to you?
_____

5. AUDIENCE IMPACT

- **Instructions** : Write a brief statement on who you want to impact with your work and how you intend to create that impact.

- **Audience:**
_____

- **Impact Statement:** I aim to impact
_____ bt
_____

6. UVP STATEMENT

- **Instructions** : Use your responses above to summarize your UVP in a concise, compelling statement.

- **UVP Statement Formula:**

- "I am a [role/expert] known for [core strengths and qualities]. I bring unique value through [key achievements and differentiators] and aim to [goal or impact aligned with audience/organizational needs]."

- **My UVP Statement:**

    "I am a _____ known for

    _____

    bring unique value through

    _____ and

    aim to

    _____

This worksheet can be revisited periodically to adjust your UVP as your career progresses, helping to ensure it remains relevant and aligned with your professional goals.

UNLOCK THE MAGIC—
SCAN, TO LEARN MORE!

CRAFTING YOUR EXECUTIVE BRAND NARRATIVE

THE ART OF STORYTELLING IN EXECUTIVE BRANDING

An executive brand is a compelling narrative embodying your identity, values, and leadership journey. It highlights not just achievements but the "why" driving your actions, building trust and emotional connection. This chapter explores storytelling techniques—clarity, relatability, and consistency—to craft an authentic narrative that inspires, connects, and enhances your influence.

1. WHY STORYTELLING MATTERS IN EXECUTIVE BRANDING

In a world where information is abundant and competition is fierce, storytelling allows you to stand out and make a lasting impression. While facts and figures are important, people remember stories. A well-crafted narrative draws people in, creating an emotional impact that lasts longer than a list of accomplishments or a polished resume. In executive branding, storytelling serves several important functions:

- **Building Trust:** Sharing your experiences openly and authentically helps build trust, a cornerstone of effective leadership.
- **Creating Connection:** Stories make you relatable. They allow others to see the human behind the title, fostering connection and engagement.
- **Reinforcing Your Unique Value:** Through storytelling, you can communicate your values, strengths, and vision in a way that resonates and sticks with your audience.

How to enhance leadership effectiveness?

Share Experience
Builds trust through authenticity.

Tell Stories
Creates connection and relatability.

Communicate Values
Reinforces unique value proposition

An executive brand narrative should aim to encapsulate who you are as a leader, why you do what you do, and how your journey and beliefs add value to your organization and industry.

2. KEY ELEMENTS OF AN EFFECTIVE EXECUTIVE BRAND NARRATIVE

A strong executive narrative is built around three essential elements: clarity, relatability, and consistency. These elements work together to refine your message, ensuring that it resonates with your audience in an authentic and effective way.

CLARITY: MAKING YOUR MESSAGE CLEAR AND FOCUSED

Clarity is vital for making your narrative impactful. A clear message communicates exactly who you are, what you stand for, and how you provide value. It ensures that your audience can easily understand your story, leaving no room for ambiguity or misinterpretation.

Techniques for Achieving Clarity:

- **Define Your Core Message:** Begin by identifying the central idea you want your narrative to convey. This could be a theme like resilience, innovation, or integrity that aligns with your unique value proposition (UVP).
- **Simplify Your Language:** Steer clear of jargon or technical terms that might distract from your message. Use straightforward language that anyone can understand.
- **Stay Focused on Key Points:** Keep your narrative focused on the most important details. A concise, well-targeted story is often more powerful than one that overflows with information.

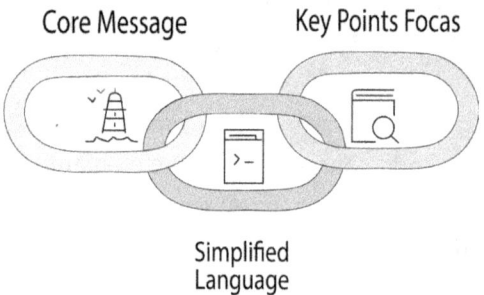

Executive Brand Narrative

Core Message | Key Points Focas | Simplified Language

Example: Consider a CEO whose career has been defined by a passion for sustainable business practices. Their core message could be: "I am committed to proving that businesses can be both profitable and environmentally responsible." This simple and clear message sets the foundation for a compelling narrative about sustainable leadership.

RELATABILITY: CONNECTING WITH YOUR AUDIENCE ON A PERSONAL LEVEL

Relatability is about making your story accessible and engaging. People who see parts of themselves in your story are more likely to trust, follow, and respect you. Relatability humanizes your leadership, making you approachable and memorable.

Techniques for Building Relatability:

- **Share Personal Experiences**: Don't just focus on your successes; share the challenges, mistakes, and lessons learned. Vulnerability can be a powerful tool in building relatability.
- **Highlight Values and Beliefs**: Make it clear what values guide your leadership and decisions. This allows your audience to connect with you on a shared foundation of values.
- **Use Everyday Language**: Avoid overly formal or rehearsed speech. Speaking naturally and with warmth makes you more relatable and fosters connection.

How to connect with the audience?

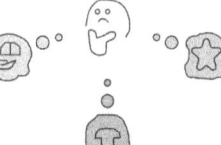

Share Personal Experiences
Builds relability through vulnerability

Highlight Values and Beliefs
Establishes a Shared foundation for connection.

Use Everyday Language
Fosters warmth and authenticity in communication.

Example: An executive who shares how a failed project taught them resilience will likely resonate with an audience. By admitting mistakes and showing growth, you demonstrate humility and openness, making your journey relatable to others who have faced similar challenges.

CONSISTENCY: ENSURING COHESION ACROSS ALL PLATFORMS

Consistency is essential in executive branding. Your narrative should be cohesive and aligned across all platforms—whether in a speech, a LinkedIn post, or a media interview. Inconsistent messaging can create confusion and weaken your brand.

Techniques for Maintaining Consistency:

- **Align with Your UVP**: Ensure each narrative element reflects your unique value proposition. Consistency in the message reinforces your core identity.
- **Use Recurrent Themes and Language**: Revisit themes, keywords, or phrases that reflect your values and expertise. Consistent language across different channels strengthens brand recall.
- **Check All Public Touchpoints**: Review your LinkedIn profile, personal website, and recent public appearances to ensure they all reflect the same narrative.

Example: If you position yourself as a data-driven leader who values transparency, ensure this message is reinforced across all channels. LinkedIn posts, company bio, and public talks should consistently reflect this narrative to solidify your brand identity.

3. STRUCTURING YOUR EXECUTIVE BRAND NARRATIVE

A well-structured narrative has a clear beginning, middle, and end. The following structure can help you create a compelling, easy-to-follow, and impactful story.

- **Beginning (The Spark):** Introduce the "spark" that sets you on your professional journey. What moment, value, or realization inspired you to embark on your current path? This could be a defining experience, a personal challenge, or an opportunity that ignited your leadership journey.
- **Example:** "My journey began when I joined a startup and witnessed first-hand the potential for technology to revolutionize healthcare. That experience ignited my passion for innovation and creating meaningful change."
- **Middle (Growth and Challenges):** Share your journey, including key achievements, challenges, and pivotal learning moments that helped shape you. This section should highlight both successes and setbacks, illustrating your resilience, adaptability, and growth.
- **Example:** "In my first executive role, I led a team through a challenging acquisition. While the experience was demanding, it taught me invaluable lessons in strategic thinking, team cohesion, and the importance of transparent communication."
- **End (Current Role and Vision for the Future):** Conclude with your current mission, values, and the impact you aspire to create. This is where you connect past experiences and lessons with your present goals, giving your audience a sense of direction and purpose.

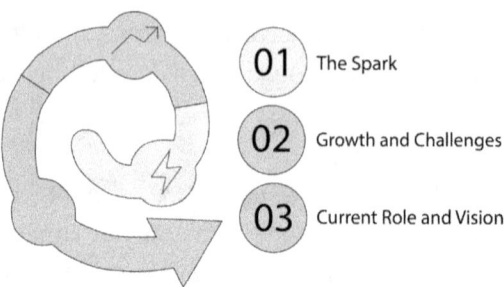

Crafting an Executive Brand narrative

01 The Spark
02 Growth and Challenges
03 Current Role and Vision

Example: "Today, as CEO of a healthcare tech company, I'm committed to making healthcare accessible through technology. My goal is to lead with integrity, pushing the boundaries of innovation while staying true to our mission of positive social impact."

4. PRACTICAL STEPS TO CRAFT AND REFINE YOUR NARRATIVE

Crafting a compelling narrative takes time and iteration. Follow these steps to refine your story:

Step 1: Draft and Reflect

> Begin by writing a rough draft of your story, following the structure outlined above. Focus on capturing the key moments and themes that define your professional journey and core values.

Step 2: Seek Feedback

> Share your draft with trusted colleagues or mentors who know you well. Ask for their input on whether the story feels authentic and whether it accurately reflects your strengths and values.

Step 3: Refine and Simplify

Based on the feedback you receive, refine your narrative. Eliminate unnecessary details and simplify the language for clarity. Ensure that each section reinforces your central message.

Step 4: Test in Different Formats

Practice delivering your narrative in various formats, such as a LinkedIn bio, a conference introduction, or a networking event. Pay attention to what resonates and make adjustments as needed.

Refine Your Executive Narrative

Practice delivering your narrative in various formats to see what resonates.

Refine and simplify
Refine your narrative by removing unnecessary details and simplifying language.

Seek Feedback
Share your draft with trusted colleages or mentors to ensure authenticity.

Draft and reflect
Being by writing a rough draft of your story, focusing on key moments and themes.

5. INCORPORATING YOUR NARRATIVE INTO YOUR BRAND TOUCHPOINTS

Your executive brand narrative—the story that conveys your values, experiences, and purpose—should be consistently communicated across all professional touchpoints. Every interaction is an opportunity to reinforce your identity, showcase your strengths, and make a lasting impression. By weaving your narrative into various platforms and presentations, you create a cohesive brand that resonates with audiences, builds credibility, and strengthens your professional presence. Here's how to incorporate your narrative effectively across key brand touchpoints.

LINKEDIN PROFILE

Your LinkedIn profile is often the first-place people visit to learn about you professionally, making it a prime platform to showcase your brand narrative. Begin with a well-crafted summary that captures your story in a few compelling paragraphs. Focus on your core values, significant career experiences, and your current mission, as well as the impact you aim to create within your industry. This summary should be concise yet powerful, offering a snapshot that helps visitors understand who you are as a leader. For example, if your career is driven by a commitment to innovation, highlight key moments where you led transformative projects, emphasizing the unique perspective you bring to the table. Ensure the language reflects your personality and tone, making your profile both professional and authentic.

COMPANY BIO

Your company bio is another crucial touchpoint, particularly for audiences who encounter you through organizational channels. Adapt your narrative to fit the format of a professional bio, focusing on your achievements, expertise, and current role. Highlight your impact within the company and how your values align with the organization's mission. For instance, if your company values innovation, emphasize your role in fostering a culture of creativity and forward-thinking. A strong company bio not only conveys your personal narrative but also reinforces your commitment to the company's vision. This alignment helps audiences view you as a dedicated leader who is both a strategic fit for your organization and a valuable asset in your field.

PUBLIC SPEAKING AND INTERVIEWS

Public speaking engagements, panels, and media interviews provide dynamic opportunities to bring your narrative to life in a personal and engaging way. When introducing yourself in these settings, incorporate elements of your narrative to create a connection with your audience. Begin with a brief story or statement that reflects your values, guiding principles, or career journey, setting the stage for your expertise. By weaving your values and vision into your responses and introductions, you reinforce your brand identity and leave a lasting impression. For example, if you're passionate about ethical leadership, mention how this commitment has shaped your career decisions and strategies. Audiences remember leaders who share authentic stories and show a clear sense of purpose, so use these opportunities to illustrate what drives you and how it shapes your approach.

ADDITIONAL TIPS FOR CONSISTENCY ACROSS TOUCHPOINTS

To build a strong, cohesive executive brand, ensure that all touchpoints consistently reflect a unified narrative. While each platform or setting may require slight adjustments in language or tone, the core message—your values, mission, and unique story—should remain consistent. Regularly review and update these touchpoints to incorporate new achievements, career shifts, or evolving goals, ensuring your brand stays current and aligned with your journey.

By embedding your brand narrative across LinkedIn, company bios, public speaking engagements, and interviews, you leave a lasting impression of a leader with clarity, purpose, and impact. This consistency not only strengthens your brand but also positions you as an authentic, values-driven leader who engages meaningfully with audiences across all professional settings.

In conclusion, crafting an engaging executive brand story is a powerful way to enhance your visibility, inspire others, and communicate your unique value. By prioritizing clarity, relatability, and consistency, you can create a narrative that deeply resonates with your audience. This story will serve as the cornerstone of your executive brand, aligning with your values and strengthening your unique value proposition across every platform and interaction. In the upcoming chapter, we will explore strategies for leveraging digital platforms to amplify your story and increase your visibility.

EXECUTIVE BRAND NARRATIVE CHECKLIST: WHERE AND HOW TO FEATURE YOUR STORY

Use this checklist to ensure your executive brand narrative reaches a broad and influential audience. From online profiles to speaking engagements, these touchpoints will amplify your story, build credibility, and open valuable connections and opportunities.

1. ONLINE PROFILES

- **LinkedIn Profile Summary:** Craft a compelling summary that highlights your core values, achievements, and vision, all while weaving in your executive brand narrative.
- **Company Website Bio:** Write a version of your story that aligns with the company's brand, focusing on your leadership role and contributions to organizational goals.

- **Professional Networking Platforms (e.g., ExecThread, AngelList):** Feature a concise version of your narrative, emphasizing your unique expertise and the value you bring to collaborations or partnerships.

2. PERSONAL WEBSITE OR PORTFOLIO

- **About Page:** Dedicate a page to your executive narrative, including your background, accomplishments, and professional mission. This helps visitors better understand your brand and leadership style.
- **Blog Section:** Write articles that expand on key elements of your story—such as career lessons or insights on industry trends. Link these back when engaging on social media or networking.
- **Case Studies or Projects Page:** Showcase specific projects or case studies that align with your story. This is a great way to demonstrate your expertise and the values you bring to each initiative.

3. CONTENT CREATION AND THOUGHT LEADERSHIP

- **Guest Articles:** Contribute articles to reputable business publications (e.g., Forbes, Inc., or Harvard Business Review) that highlight your story, expertise, and industry insights. This positions you as a thought leader and boosts visibility for your brand.
- **Personal Blog Posts:** Publish posts that reflect on milestones in your career or your values-driven leadership. Consistently posting will help you build an engaged audience over time.
- **LinkedIn Articles:** Share articles on LinkedIn that highlight aspects of your executive journey, leadership philosophy, or outlook on industry trends. These articles can foster organic reach and engagement from peers. Consider creating a LinkedIn newsletter to share these insights regularly.

4. PODCASTS AND MEDIA APPEARANCES

- **Guest on Industry Podcasts:** Reach out to podcasts relevant to your industry or leadership style. Share your story and insights, allowing listeners to connect with your brand on a personal level.
- **Start Your Own Podcast:** Hosting your own podcast lets you share your journey over time and connect with other leaders. This is a great way to build an audience while also making valuable connections.
- **Webinars and Video Interviews:** Participate in webinars or video interviews where you can discuss your expertise, leadership insights, and personal journey. These may be hosted by your organization, industry groups, or other leaders in the field.

5. SOCIAL MEDIA AND ONLINE ENGAGEMENT

- **Social Media Profiles (LinkedIn, Twitter):** Regularly share snippets of your story, reflections on career moments, or updates about your current work. Engage with others in your field to build a following and connect with potential collaborators.
- **Instagram or Facebook Live:** Host live sessions where your audience is active, sharing parts of your story or answering questions related to your expertise.
- **Regular LinkedIn Updates:** Share weekly or monthly reflections that relate back to your story and brand. This can include recent achievements, lessons learned, or valuable insights into your industry.

6. SPEAKING OPPORTUNITIES AND PUBLIC ENGAGEMENTS

- **Industry Conferences:** Look for speaking opportunities at conferences where you can share your narrative, leadership insights, and vision. Position yourself as an expert speaker on topics that align with your story.
- **Company and Community Events:** Participate in internal company events or community panels to share your story with colleagues, clients, or local audiences.
- **Professional Associations and Networking Groups:** Join associations relevant to your industry, where you can give talks or presentations that highlight your journey, unique skills, and leadership philosophy.

7. EDUCATIONAL CONTENT AND WORKSHOPS

- **Guest Lecturer:** Volunteer as a guest speaker at universities, business schools, or industry training programs, using your story to inspire and educate emerging professionals.
- **Host Workshops or Masterclasses:** Offer workshops focused on your areas of expertise, naturally incorporating your personal story and professional journey.
- **Webinars:** Host webinars centered on topics that align with your story, sharing personal insights and industry knowledge, allowing attendees to connect with your brand on a deeper level.

8. COMMUNITY INVOLVEMENT AND BOARD SERVICE

- **Non-Profit Board Positions:** Serving on a non-profit board is a powerful way to reinforce your values and commitment to community impact, which is often an essential part of an executive narrative.

- **Community Panels or Local Events:** Participate in community-focused panels or events where you can share your story and engage with a broader audience.
- **Professional Mentorship:** Offer mentorship programs to share your experience with others, demonstrating your commitment to guiding the next generation of leaders.

9. WRITTEN PUBLICATIONS

- **Author a Book or E-Book:** If your story and perspective are strong, consider writing a book to share your journey, insights, and leadership philosophy. This is an excellent way to establish authority and reach a wider audience.
- **Case Studies or White Papers:** Publish case studies or white papers that reflect on lessons from your career and unique approaches to overcoming challenges. This will demonstrate your expertise and add depth to your story.

10. NETWORKING AND ONE-ON-ONE OPPORTUNITIES

- **Professional Networking Events:** At networking events, briefly share your story in your introductions to create a memorable first impression.
- **Virtual Coffee Chats:** Host virtual or in-person coffee chats with industry peers, using your story to connect and inspire potential collaborators.
- **Alumni Associations:** Participate in alumni events or newsletters to share career highlights or leadership stories, helping you stay connected to your network.

CHECKLIST SUMMARY

Preparation Steps:

- Write a concise executive narrative (bio or "About Me" section) that captures your story.
- Identify platforms where your story can be shared authentically and strategically.
- Create a content calendar for social media, articles, and podcasts to share elements of your narrative regularly.

Engagement Steps:

- Pitch yourself to relevant podcasts, blogs, or publications as a guest expert.
- Attend and speak at industry conferences and networking events.
- Explore public and community engagement avenues, such as mentorship, board service, and webinars.

Action Steps:

- Start or appear on podcasts, publish guest articles, and build relationships within your industry.
- Incorporate your narrative into LinkedIn updates, webinars, and thought leadership content.
- Use consistent language and themes across all touchpoints to maintain a cohesive brand presence.

By following this checklist and leveraging multiple platforms to share your story, you'll be able to create a strong, visible, and memorable executive brand that establishes you as a thought leader and fosters meaningful connections.

UNLOCK THE MAGIC—
SCAN, TO LEARN MORE!

5
BUILDING AN ONLINE PRESENCE

THE IMPORTANCE OF A STRONG ONLINE PRESENCE FOR EXECUTIVES

An executive brand is a powerful narrative reflecting your identity, values, and leadership journey. It conveys not just achievements but the "why" behind them, fostering trust and connection. This chapter examines storytelling techniques—clarity, relatability, and consistency—to craft an authentic narrative that inspires and amplifies your influence.

1. CORE DIGITAL STRATEGIES FOR ENHANCING VISIBILITY

Building an impactful online presence is crucial for executives to expand influence, connect with key audiences, and strengthen their brand by thoughtfully curating platforms aligned with professional goals and audiences, ensuring a consistent, engaging digital footprint.

CHOOSE PLATFORMS WISELY

While LinkedIn is the go-to platform for professionals and executives, expanding your reach by creating content on secondary platforms can enhance your brand's visibility. Each platform has a unique audience and tone, so select those that complement your messaging style. For example, YouTube and Instagram are ideal for sharing video content, allowing you to connect with audiences personally. Twitter effectively shares insights, updates, and engages in industry conversations. Consider where your target audience spends time and choose platforms that support your brand's voice and goals.

MAINTAIN CONSISTENT BRANDING

Consistency is essential for creating a cohesive online identity. Use the same profile photo, bio, and background information across all platforms to ensure that your brand remains unified and recognizable.

A professional headshot that reflects both your personal style and your brand is crucial, as is a well-crafted bio that clearly conveys your expertise, values, and current role. Maintaining consistent branding reinforces your credibility and makes it easier for others to recognize and trust you across different platforms.

ENGAGE REGULARLY

Having an active presence is key to building connections and staying relevant. Simply having a profile isn't enough; active engagement with your audience is essential. Share insights, articles, and updates relevant to your industry, and take the time to respond thoughtfully to comments on your posts. Interact with others by liking, commenting on, and sharing content from peers or industry leaders. Engaging in discussions and maintaining an active presence keeps your profile visible and positions you as an approachable, engaged leader.

LEVERAGE MULTIMEDIA CONTENT

Multimedia content is a powerful way to capture attention and deepen engagement. Video content, in particular, lets you showcase your personality and communicate directly with your audience. Use platforms like YouTube and Instagram to share videos on industry trends, leadership tips, or behind-the-scenes insights into your professional life. Additionally, consider using infographics, slideshows, or images to reinforce your message. Visual content is highly engaging and shareable, making it an excellent tool for expanding your reach and connecting with your audience in a memorable way.

By curating a strategic online presence across selected platforms, maintaining consistent branding, engaging regularly, and incorporating multimedia content, you can build a powerful digital footprint that strengthens your executive brand. This approach will help you connect authentically with your audience, amplify your message, and build credibility as a leader who understands and leverages the power of digital influence.

BUILDING AND OPTIMIZING YOUR LINKEDIN PROFILE

LinkedIn is the ultimate platform for executives, providing a dynamic and versatile space to showcase your professional background, achievements, and expertise. With over 700 million professionals on the platform, LinkedIn serves as a networking hub that connects executives with peers, recruiters, and potential collaborators worldwide. An optimized LinkedIn profile acts as a digital resume, a thought leadership platform, and a networking tool all in one, greatly enhancing your credibility, visibility, and influence. Here, we'll guide you through the process of building and refining each element of your LinkedIn profile to create a compelling and impactful executive brand.

2. WHY LINKEDIN IS ESSENTIAL FOR EXECUTIVES

LinkedIn is more than just a social media platform—it's a powerful tool that enables executives to establish a professional brand rooted in credibility, expertise, and industry insight. For leaders seeking to expand their influence, connect with industry peers, and attract high-level opportunities, LinkedIn provides a strategic advantage that surpasses traditional networking methods. Here's how LinkedIn can elevate an executive's brand and open up new professional opportunities.

SHOWCASE CAREER ACHIEVEMENTS

An optimized LinkedIn profile serves as a dynamic, accessible portfolio that highlights your career accomplishments, experience, and unique value proposition. With sections dedicated to career history, skills, awards, projects, and recommendations, LinkedIn provides a comprehensive view of your professional journey. For executives, this visibility is invaluable—it enables industry peers, recruiters, and potential collaborators to quickly grasp your achievements. Including quantifiable results, impactful projects, and leadership roles further enhances credibility, presenting your expertise in an authentic and compelling way.

BUILD THOUGHT LEADERSHIP

LinkedIn is ideal for establishing thought leadership by sharing insights and expertise. Executives can post updates, publish articles, or use LinkedIn's newsletter feature to share perspectives on industry trends, best practices, or personal leadership philosophies. Consistent content sharing not only demonstrates expertise but also helps build a dedicated following of professionals who look to you for guidance. Engaging in conversations around your posts boosts visibility and strengthens your position as an active, influential voice in your field.

EXPAND NETWORKS

LinkedIn is a powerful platform for expanding professional networks, allowing executives to connect with peers, mentors, clients, and industry leaders. It offers fresh ideas, collaborations, and opportunities for growth. Its features, like "People You May Know," groups, and messaging tools, foster valuable connections that enhance business and career development.

ATTRACT OPPORTUNITIES

With its advanced search tools, LinkedIn has become a go-to resource for recruiters and industry professionals seeking executive talent. Executives who optimize their profiles with relevant keywords, concise summaries, and clear descriptions of their expertise increase their chances of being discovered for consulting, board, and senior leadership roles. A well-curated LinkedIn profile signals active engagement in your industry, making it more likely that companies, recruiters, and potential clients will reach out with valuable opportunities.

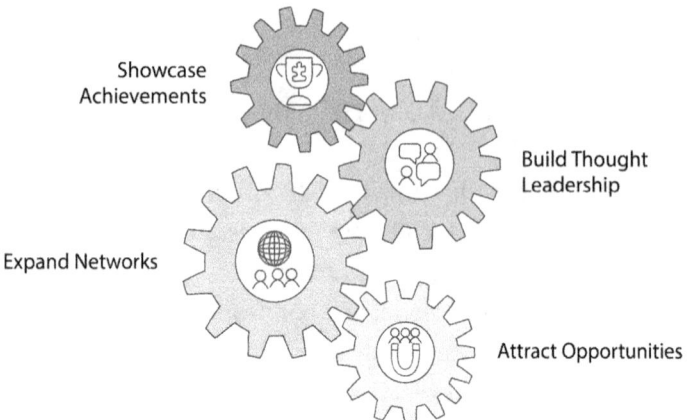

By leveraging LinkedIn as a key element of your executive brand, you can highlight your career achievements, establish thought leadership, expand your professional network, and attract new opportunities. LinkedIn's unique ability to combine visibility, credibility, and networking enables executives to take control of their professional image, positioning themselves for sustained growth and influence within their industries.

LET'S EXPLORE EACH SECTION OF A LINKEDIN PROFILE AND HOW TO MAXIMIZE ITS POTENTIAL.

1. PROFILE IMAGE AND BACKGROUND IMAGE

PROFILE IMAGE

- **Purpose**: The profile image is the first visual visitors see and plays a crucial role in establishing trust and professionalism.
- **Optimization Tips:**

- **Invest in a Professional Photoshoot**: Quality matters. Find a local photographer who can capture a polished, high-resolution headshot.
- **Choose Appropriate Attire and Expression**: Dress in professional attire that reflects your industry. A confident, approachable expression works best for creating an inviting impression.
- **Use a Plain or Neutral Background**: A clean background avoids distractions and keeps the focus on you.

BACKGROUND IMAGE (BANNER)

- **Purpose**: The background image is a valuable yet often overlooked branding opportunity. It can visually convey your expertise, values, or professional environment.
- **Optimization Tips**:
- **Highlight Your Brand**: Use a custom banner that showcases your organization's logo, industry-relevant imagery, or a tagline that reflects your unique value proposition.
- **Showcase Achievements**: If you're a public speaker or have received industry awards, consider featuring visuals that hint at these accomplishments.
- **Use High-Quality Images**: Avoid low-resolution images, as they can detract from the professionalism of your profile.

2. HEADLINE

The LinkedIn headline is one of the most critical elements, as it appears prominently in search results and is often the deciding factor for profile clicks.

- **Purpose**: The headline should capture your leadership essence, highlighting your role, industry, and unique strengths.
- **Optimization Tips**:

- **Go Beyond Job Titles**: Instead of a generic title, convey what makes you unique. For instance, instead of "CEO of Tech Innovations," try "CEO of Tech Innovations | Driving Digital Transformation & Sustainable Growth."
- **Incorporate Relevant Keywords**: Use keywords related to your expertise to increase searchability, such as "AI Strategy," "Global Leadership," or "Healthcare Transformation."
- **Highlight Key Achievements or Values**: Consider adding a brief phrase that reflects your mission, such as "Champion of Diversity in Tech" or "Passionate About Sustainable Business Solutions."

3. ABOUT SECTION

The About section is an opportunity to tell your story, communicate your unique value proposition, and demonstrate what makes you a valuable leader in your industry.

- **Purpose**: To provide a narrative about your career journey, leadership philosophy, and professional mission.
- **Optimization Tips**:
- **Start Strong**: Capture attention with a powerful opening that introduces your unique value proposition and the impact you aim to make in your field.
- **Share Key Achievements**: Highlight pivotal moments, awards, or milestones in your career to showcase your expertise and accomplishments.
- **Use First-Person**: Writing in the first person makes your About section feel personal and authentic.
- **Conclude with a Call to Action**: Encourage visitors to connect, explore your articles, or reach out for collaboration. This can be as simple as "Let's connect if you're passionate about [industry expertise or goal]."

4. EXPERIENCE AND EDUCATION SECTION

EXPERIENCE

The Experience section allows you to chronologically showcase your career, giving context to each role and enabling you to highlight specific contributions and results.

- **Purpose**: To give a detailed view of your professional journey, focusing on your achievements, growth, and impact.
- **Optimization Tips:**
- **Provide Measurable Results**: Include data-driven achievements wherever possible (e.g., "Led a team that increased revenue by 30% in two years").
- **Focus on Leadership and Impact**: Highlight the specific impact of your leadership, such as launching new initiatives, transforming team culture, or spearheading innovation.
- **Add Media and Links**: Use LinkedIn's media feature to add links, images, or presentations to provide additional context and showcase projects or case studies.

EDUCATION

- **Why It Matters**: Your educational background adds credibility, particularly if you have specialized training or degrees relevant to your industry.
- **Best Practices**:
- List all degrees, certifications, and professional training relevant to your career.
- Mention any honors or distinctions, and consider including additional coursework if it aligns with your expertise.

5. SKILLS & ENDORSEMENTS

THE SKILLS & ENDORSEMENTS SECTION OFFERS SOCIAL PROOF OF YOUR EXPERTISE AND AREAS OF STRENGTH.

- **Purpose**: To validate your expertise through endorsements from connections and align your skills with your executive brand.
- **Optimization Tips:**
- **Prioritize Key Skills**: List skills that align with your expertise and UVP, ideally those most relevant to your industry and current role.
- **Encourage Endorsements**: Politely ask trusted colleagues or peers to endorse specific skills that reflect your unique strengths.
- **Highlight Leadership Skills**: Include skills like "Strategic Leadership," "Change Management," and "Innovation" that emphasize your capabilities as an executive.

6. PUBLICATIONS, PROJECTS, HONORS & AWARDS AND LANGUAGES

These sections boost credibility, showcasing your thought leadership and recognition in your field.

PUBLICATIONS

- **Purpose**: To feature articles, books, or research you've authored, establishing you as a thought leader.
- **Optimization Tips:**
- **Link to External Content**: Include links to articles published on reputable platforms like Forbes, Inc., or your company's blog.
- **Summarize the Publication's Value**: Add a brief description of what the publication covers and why it's relevant to your audience.

PROJECTS

- **Purpose:** To highlight major projects you've led or contributed to that align with your expertise.
- **Optimization Tips:**
- **Describe Each Project's Impact:** Focus on the results of each project, whether that's revenue growth, process improvement, or product innovation.
- **Add Collaborators:** If appropriate, tag colleagues or partners to enhance credibility and showcase teamwork.

HONORS & AWARDS

- **Purpose:** To showcase industry recognition that reinforces your authority and influence.
- **Optimization Tips:**
- **Highlight Relevant Awards:** List awards that directly relate to your expertise and achievements, such as "Top 40 Under 40 in Healthcare."
- **Add Context:** Briefly explain the significance of each award if it isn't widely recognized.

VOLUNTEER EXPERIENCE

- **Why It Matters:** Volunteering shows your commitment to causes and adds depth to your professional persona.
- **Best Practices:**
- Include volunteer roles that align with your personal values or industry, as these reflect positively on your character and community engagement.

LANGUAGES

- **Why It Matters**: Multilingual executives often bring unique cultural insights to their roles.
- **Best Practices**:
- Include languages you speak fluently or proficiently.
- Be honest about your skill level, as language skills can come into play in international roles or opportunities.

7. LINKEDIN NEWSLETTER

LinkedIn's newsletter feature is a powerful way for executives to share insights, industry trends, and thought leadership with an engaged audience.

- **Purpose**: To create a regular stream of value-driven content that builds relationships with your network and positions you as a trusted voice.
- **Optimization Tips**:
- **Establish a Consistent Publishing Schedule**: Weekly or monthly updates help keep you on your mind for your connections.
- **Provide Actionable Insights**: Focus on topics that offer valuable takeaways for your audience, whether leadership tips, industry trends, or strategic insights.
- **Cross-Promote**: Share links to your newsletter on other social media channels to increase subscribers and engagement.

8. RECOMMENDATIONS

Recommendations offer personal testimonials from your connections, reinforcing your skills, work ethic, and impact.

- **Purpose**: To validate your expertise and leadership qualities with credible, third-party validation.
- **Optimization Tips**:

- **Seek Recommendations from Peers, Mentors, and Reports**: Request feedback from individuals who have firsthand experience working with you, covering a range of perspectives.
- **Write Genuine Recommendations for Others**: Reciprocating with meaningful recommendations can strengthen relationships and lead to mutual endorsements.

9. BUILDING ENGAGEMENT THROUGH LINKEDIN ACTIVITY

A well-built LinkedIn profile alone isn't enough; active engagement helps keep your profile visible and builds credibility.

- **Post Regularly**: Share insights, industry news, or reflections on recent events relevant to your audience.
- **Comment Thoughtfully**: Engaging with others' posts, especially those of industry leaders, helps build visibility and positions you as an engaged member of the community.
- **Join and Participate in Groups**: LinkedIn Groups provide additional networking opportunities. Join groups relevant to your industry and participate in discussions.
- **Cross-Promote Content**: Share articles, blog posts, and achievements from other platforms (such as YouTube videos or publications) to increase exposure and engagement.

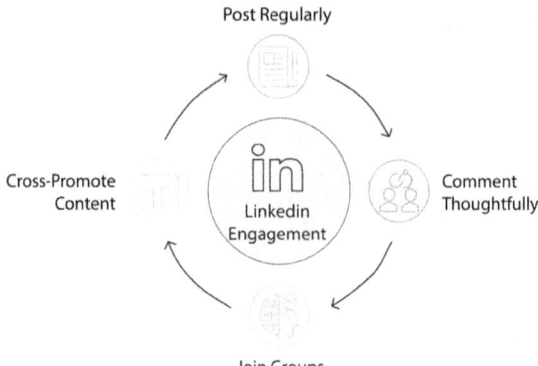

An optimized LinkedIn profile serves as the backbone of your online presence. Each profile component—from your headline and About section to the newsletter feature and recommendations—should work together to present a cohesive, compelling narrative showcasing your leadership, accomplishments, and unique value. Building an active, well-curated LinkedIn profile can significantly enhance your professional credibility and open doors to new opportunities, partnerships, and growth.

3. SOCIAL MEDIA ENGAGEMENT ACROSS PLATFORMS

While LinkedIn is essential, building an executive brand can be strengthened by engaging on additional platforms that resonate with your target audience. Each social media platform serves a unique purpose and can help amplify your message to a broader audience.

YOUTUBE AND YOUTUBE SHORTS

- **Why It Matters**: YouTube is highly engaging and allows you to showcase expertise through videos. YouTube Shorts, in particular, offer quick, digestible content that can reach a wider audience.
- **Best Practices**:

- Share leadership insights, industry trends, or "behind the scenes" content.
- Use Shorts for quick tips, motivational messages, or summaries of longer content.
- Engage with comments to connect directly with your viewers.

INSTAGRAM

- **Why It Matters**: Instagram humanizes your brand and allows you to connect more personally, especially through visual content.
- **Best Practices**:
- Share snapshots of your work life, achievements, and events.
- Use Stories and Reels to give quick insights into your day-to-day or share thoughts on relevant topics.
- Cross-promote LinkedIn articles or achievements in Instagram posts.

FACEBOOK

- **Why It Matters**: Facebook can support networking and industry engagement, especially through groups.
- **Best Practices**:
- Share updates on recent articles, achievements, or speaking engagements.
- Join industry-related Facebook groups to connect with peers and share insights.
- Post links to your LinkedIn newsletter to encourage cross-platform engagement.

TIKTOK

- **Why It Matters**: While TikTok may not seem immediately relevant, it's becoming a place for professional insights, especially for reaching younger demographics.

- **Best Practices**:
- Use TikTok for short, engaging content on industry insights, leadership tips, or career advice.
- Experiment with educational content that's quick and impactful, using visuals and storytelling.

4. BEST PRACTICES FOR ONLINE ENGAGEMENT

Once your profiles are set up, it's crucial to maintain active engagement to grow your visibility and credibility.

- **Consistency is Key**: Regularly post and engage across all platforms to keep your brand at the forefront of your mind.
- **Content Sharing**: Share articles, industry news, and relevant insights. Curate content that aligns with your brand and positions you as an informed leader.
- **Engage with Your Audience**: Respond to comments, messages, and reactions. Engagement shows approachability and builds relationships with your network.
- **Cross-Promotion**: Link content from one platform to another, like sharing your LinkedIn posts on Twitter or promoting your YouTube videos on LinkedIn. This helps your followers find you across platforms.
- **Track and Adjust**: Use analytics tools to measure the performance of your content. Adjust your strategies based on what resonates most with your audience.

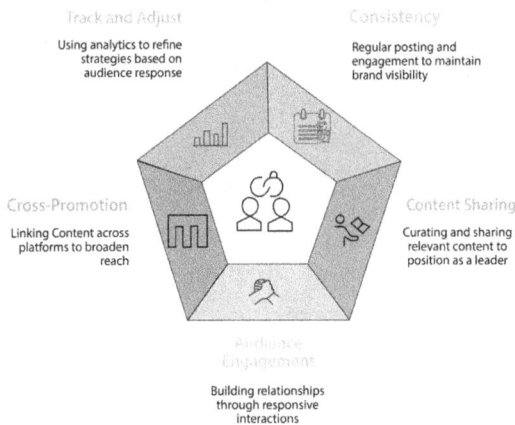

5. AMPLIFYING YOUR BRAND THROUGH A PERSONAL WEBSITE

A personal website is an invaluable asset for any executive seeking to build a strong, cohesive online presence. Serving as a central hub, your website provides a space where you can showcase your brand in a controlled, customizable environment. It allows you to highlight your expertise, share valuable content, and connect with your audience directly. Unlike social media profiles, a personal website is entirely yours, offering the flexibility to tell your story and build authority on your terms. Below are essential sections to include on your website to ensure it effectively amplifies and supports your executive brand.

ABOUT ME

The "About Me" section of your website offers a unique opportunity to expand on your LinkedIn profile summary, providing a more detailed look into your career journey, values, and goals. This section should reflect your personal story, spotlight pivotal moments in your career, and underscore the principles that define your leadership. For instance, if you're passionate about innovation and transformation, share anecdotes that demonstrate how these values have shaped your professional path. By offering visitors a deeper insight into who you are, the "About Me" section creates a connection that's both personal and professional, setting the tone for the rest of your site.

BLOG

A blog is a dynamic feature that allows you to regularly share fresh insights, lessons learned, and commentary on industry trends. By publishing articles that showcase your expertise, experiences, and unique perspective, you position yourself as a thought leader actively contributing to discussions within your field. A well-maintained blog signals that you're engaged with current issues, adaptable to change, and committed to sharing valuable knowledge. Consistently posting high-quality content—whether on leadership, innovation, or other key topics—ensures your audience returns for more, positioning your website as a trusted resource for industry insights.

MEDIA AND PUBLICATIONS

The "Media and Publications" section serves as an online portfolio, featuring links to your published articles, videos, podcast appearances, and speaking engagements. This collection of work reinforces your credibility and demonstrates the breadth of your influence across various media channels. Including links or embedded content makes it easy for visitors to access your thought leadership, while also providing tangible proof of your expertise. Be sure to keep this section updated as you continue to contribute to new outlets, ensuring your audience stays informed of your latest accomplishments and contributions.

CONTACT INFORMATION

A well-designed contact section simplifies the process for others to reach out for professional opportunities—whether it's for speaking engagements, networking, consulting, or collaboration. Include a professional email address or a contact form that directs inquiries to your inbox, along with any relevant social media links. If you're open to public speaking or board appointments, consider specifying the areas of interest that best align with your expertise, giving potential partners a clearer understanding of how you can contribute. Offering easily accessible and inviting contact details signals openness and strengthens your willingness to engage with others meaningfully.

By including these key sections, your personal website becomes a comprehensive platform that reflects your leadership style, shares your insights, and facilitates meaningful connections with your audience. This dedicated space allows you to tell your story, build credibility, and make lasting impressions that enhance your professional reputation and online presence. As an extension of your executive brand, a personal website gives you the freedom and control to amplify your influence and make a significant impact across the digital landscape.

Keep in mind:

Building a robust online presence requires ongoing commitment across multiple platforms. For executives, LinkedIn serves as the foundation of your digital brand, but a carefully crafted presence on other platforms can further elevate your influence and credibility. By implementing these strategies, you'll create a polished, compelling, and prominent online presence that strengthens your personal brand and expands your reach as a leader.

5B

HOW TO USE AI WITH LINKEDIN AUTHENTICALLY - BY JOE APFELBAUM CEO OF EVYAI

As a board member, using LinkedIn regularly is essential. Executives want to see that you take your personal brand seriously—it reflects professionalism and shows you care about your reputation.

When I search for executives and leaders on Google, LinkedIn profiles often appear on the first page of results. In many cases, it's the very first result.

This chapter explores how to leverage AI in conjunction with LinkedIn to sound authentic while maximizing the platform's potential.

WHY LINKEDIN MATTERS

I've been using LinkedIn since 2006, but I began taking it seriously only after Microsoft acquired it for $26.2 billion and committed to making it the top professional social network. Today, LinkedIn boasts over a billion users, with the CEO aiming for three billion. Optimizing your profile, posting, engaging, messaging, and building your presence has never been more important.

Networking has brought me my greatest opportunities. It's because of LinkedIn that I'm writing this chapter, and you're reading it.

Millions of people see my activity on LinkedIn, but through this chapter, I get to build a personal connection with you—a testament to LinkedIn's power. Over the past decade, I've educated thousands of professionals on how to maximize LinkedIn's potential. Now, let me guide you through the key areas to focus on for the best results.

If you'd like to see my profile, visit www.linkedin.com/in/joeapfelbaum. I don't just teach LinkedIn—I live it.

YOUR LINKEDIN PROFILE: MORE IMPORTANT THAN YOUR WEBSITE

Why is your LinkedIn profile more critical than your website?

Because while anyone can create a website, your LinkedIn profile is verified. You can authenticate it using your ID at www.linkedin.com/verify.

Your profile includes your name, photo, recommendations (which serve as social proof), and mutual connections—all of which build trust. Additionally, LinkedIn notifies you when someone views your profile, enabling proactive engagement.

For instance, if the CEO of a major company looks at my profile, I don't wait for them to reach out. Instead, I take the initiative to invite them to connect.

CRAFTING THE PERFECT CONNECTION NOTE

When reaching out, I use AI to craft customized, context-rich connection notes. This increases trust and connection—key factors in achieving a higher acceptance rate.

I follow the "3 Cs" of connection notes: Customize, Contextualize, and Connect.

With evyAI, crafting the perfect connection note takes just three seconds. You simply select your goal, tone, and persona, then generate the note. It's that simple.

EXPANDING YOUR NETWORK

I recommend connecting with three types of people:

- Prospective clients
- Centers of influence
- Engaged LinkedIn users who can amplify your content

Did you know that every LinkedIn connection also becomes a follower? This means adding 10,000 connections translates into 10,000 followers. Despite this, most executives have only 440 connections, and the average CEO has just 930.

IF MORE EXECUTIVES UNDERSTOOD THIS, THEY COULD EASILY GROW THEIR NETWORK BY CONNECTING WITH 20 NEW PEOPLE DAILY. WITH AI TOOLS, SENDING 20 CONNECTION NOTES TAKES LESS THAN FIVE MINUTES.

WHAT'S NEXT AFTER ADDING CONNECTIONS?

After connecting, focus on three daily activities to gain exposure, credibility, and conversations:

Post Regularly: If your goal is exposure, post often. LinkedIn posts typically reach 100–1,000 views, compared to 10 views for tweets on X.

- **Pro Tip: Avoid including links in your post, as LinkedIn deprioritizes posts that direct users off-platform. Instead, share links in the comments.**

Engage Thoughtfully: Comment on others' posts to build visibility and relationships.

Send Messages: Use personalized messages to foster meaningful connections.

AI-POWERED POSTING

Use AI to craft compelling posts that include:

- **A Hook**
- **Main Points**
- **A Call to Action**
- **Three Hashtags**

With tools like evyAI, creating engaging content becomes effortless.

JOIN THE COMMUNITY

For additional prompts, templates, and LinkedIn hacks, join our AI for LinkedIn community at www.skool.com/evyai.

HOW OFTEN SHOULD YOU POST ON LINKEDIN?

We recommend posting once a day. LinkedIn posts gain the most visibility in the first 24 hours before their reach diminishes. Videos, however, tend to have a longer visibility window, while polls remain visible for the duration of the poll.

Include keywords in your posts that your target audience is likely to search for. While LinkedIn posts don't rank on Google, LinkedIn articles rank exceptionally well.

If you're aiming for SEO, publish at least one 2000-word article each month. This article can serve as your content pillar, inspiring multiple posts.

Need post ideas? Use AI tools like the evyAI idea generator to brainstorm topics. Once you have a topic, you can draft your post in seconds using AI. Be sure to review and refine the post to enhance its quality—AI is here to assist, not replace, your unique voice.

LEVERAGING AI TO ENHANCE YOUR LINKEDIN PRESENCE

When creating a post, instruct the AI on your desired tone, goal, and persona. Building an AI persona that mirrors your style is key to producing content that aligns with your voice. Provide examples of your content and specify words to avoid (e.g., "unlock," "synergy"). For a conversational tone, ask AI to craft posts that feel like chatting with a friend.

You can create separate personas for your personal profile and company pages, enabling tailored content for each audience. Remember, LinkedIn allows one personal profile but multiple company pages. A helpful tip: like and comment on your own posts from your company pages to boost engagement.

STRATEGIES TO INCREASE ENGAGEMENT ON LINKEDIN

Engagement is critical for LinkedIn's algorithm, especially in the first hour after posting. To encourage interaction:

Engage with others' content. Why would someone engage with your post if you don't engage with theirs? Dedicate a few minutes daily to comment on at least five posts.

Target strategic connections. Save profiles of key contacts (e.g., advocates, collaborators, clients) in evyAI and group them into lists for easy access.

Focus on posts with zero comments. Leaving comments on unengaged posts can increase visibility and build goodwill.

We provide a link to find posts with no comments in the evyAI Learning Hub—a valuable resource for our clients.

BUILDING RELATIONSHIPS THROUGH DIRECT MESSAGING

Avoid using LinkedIn DMs for direct sales—it's the equivalent of shoving a business card in someone's face at a networking event. Instead, focus on relationship-building and offering value. Use LinkedIn's "Catch Up" tab to send personalized messages for birthdays, anniversaries, or new roles.

For crafting messages, evyAI can assist by generating highly customized texts. You can also use its mic feature to dictate messages, making it quick and efficient. Sending 10 thoughtful messages daily can help you stay top of mind with your network.

OPTIMIZING YOUR LINKEDIN PROFILE

Increased activity will drive more profile views. Ensure your profile makes a strong first impression by focusing on:

- **Photo and background banner:** Use tools like Canva for professional, eye-catching banners.
- **Headline and About section:** Let AI help you craft concise and impactful text.
- **Featured posts and experience sections:** Highlight relevant content to showcase your expertise.

BUILDING AND RECEIVING RECOMMENDATIONS

Recommendations strengthen your profile. To get more:
- Write recommendations for others—they're likely to reciprocate.
- Ask satisfied clients for recommendations based on their feedback.
- Make it easy by requesting recommendations directly through LinkedIn. Include a personalized note to guide their response.
- With AI, crafting recommendations is quick and straightforward. Though recommendations can be time-consuming to write, they are invaluable for building credibility.

CONTRIBUTING AS A THOUGHT LEADER

Contribute to collaborative articles on LinkedIn (www.linkedin.com/advice). These articles are AI-generated, so using AI to refine your contributions is both efficient and acceptable. Make sure to apply the appropriate persona to align your contributions with your desired tone and style.

By posting consistently, engaging strategically, and leveraging tools like evyAI, you can elevate your LinkedIn presence and become a thought leader in your field. Remember, success on LinkedIn is about creating value, building relationships, and showcasing your expertise.

UNLOCK THE MAGIC—
SCAN, TO LEARN MORE!

6

NETWORKING AND RELATIONSHIP BUILDING

THE IMPORTANCE OF NETWORKING IN EXECUTIVE BRANDING

Networking is an essential skill for executives, connecting you with peers, mentors, potential collaborators, and industry leaders who can significantly impact your career growth and influence. A robust network transcends immediate business opportunities, offering a support system of trusted advisors, opening doors to innovative ideas, and amplifying your influence within your industry. Effective networking is not about amassing contacts; it's about fostering meaningful relationships that drive mutual growth and success.

In this chapter, we'll explore key strategies for both in-person and online networking to help you build a vibrant, supportive, and strategically valuable network. We'll also discuss ways to nurture these connections over time, ensuring your relationships remain mutually beneficial and reinforce your executive brand.

WHY NETWORKING IS ESSENTIAL FOR EXECUTIVES

For executives, networking is more than just advantageous—it's indispensable. Here's a closer look at how networking can profoundly impact your career and enhance your ability to lead effectively:

1. ACCESS TO PEERS AND INDUSTRY INSIGHTS

- **Connecting with Peers:** Networking enables you to connect with other leaders who face similar challenges and opportunities, creating a community of peers who understand the unique demands of high-level roles. These connections can act as sounding boards, helping you refine ideas and strategies.

- **Staying Informed:** Your network provides access to the latest industry insights, trends, and best practices. Engaging with others in your field keeps you informed about emerging technologies, competitive strategies, and market shifts, ensuring you remain ahead of the curve.

2. MENTORSHIP AND GUIDANCE

- **Learning from Mentors:** Networking introduces you to potential mentors who have successfully navigated challenges similar to yours. Their advice, lessons learned, and guidance can accelerate your growth and help you avoid common pitfalls.
- **Providing Mentorship:** Building your network also gives you opportunities to mentor rising leaders. Mentoring strengthens your leadership abilities, reinforces your expertise, and broadens your influence by shaping the next generation of executives.

3. OPPORTUNITIES FOR COLLABORATION AND GROWTH

- **Identifying Collaborators:** Networking unlocks potential collaborations, partnerships, and strategic alliances that can propel organizational growth. You may discover partners whose skills complement yours, who share your vision, or who have resources to enhance your impact.
- **Uncovering New Roles or Board Positions:** Many executive opportunities—such as board seats, consulting roles, or new leadership positions—are filled through recommendations within trusted networks. A strong network increases your visibility, positioning you as a prime candidate when these opportunities arise.

4. SUPPORT SYSTEM OF TRUSTED ADVISORS

- **Building a Safety Net:** Executive roles often bring unique pressures and challenges. A trusted network of advisors provides a safe space for candid discussions, helping you navigate complex situations with confidence. Their objective perspectives enable you to make well-informed decisions.
- **Establishing Credibility and Influence:** A well-established network endorses your expertise and leadership. Relationships with reputable professionals bolster your credibility and enhance your influence within your industry.

5. OPENING DOORS TO INNOVATION AND NEW IDEAS

- **Exposure to Diverse Perspectives:** Networking exposes you to ideas and viewpoints that may differ from your own, sparking creativity and innovation. These interactions often inspire new approaches, products, or strategies that you might not have considered independently.
- **Learning Across Industries:** Networking extends beyond your industry. Cross-sector connections provide insights into how other fields address similar challenges, offering innovative solutions you can adapt to your own context.

6. ENHANCED PERSONAL AND PROFESSIONAL GROWTH

- **Accountability and Personal Growth:** Trusted connections foster accountability and personal development, offering constructive feedback to help you refine your leadership style and enhance your effectiveness.
- **Increased Resilience and Adaptability:** Learning from others' experiences with adversity builds resilience. Their stories of overcoming challenges can prepare you to face your own with a more adaptable, solution-focused mindset.

By mastering the art of networking, you can build and sustain relationships that empower you to lead with confidence, innovate effectively, and achieve your long-term career goals.

Benefits of Executive Networking

Personal Growth
Encouraging accountability and resilence

Access to Peers
Connecting with industry leaders for shared insights

Innovation Exposure
Gaining new ideas from diverse perspectives

Mentorship Opportunities
Building relationships for guidance and growth

Support System
Establishing a network of trusted advisors

Collaboration Opportunities
Finding partners for strategic alliances

EFFECTIVE NETWORKING: BEYOND COLLECTING CONTACTS

Networking is more than compiling a list of names and titles—it's about building meaningful, mutually beneficial, and sustainable relationships. Here's how to move beyond collecting contacts and cultivate impactful connections:

1. FOCUS ON RELATIONSHIP BUILDING, NOT TRANSACTIONAL CONNECTIONS

- **Invest Time and Effort:** Effective networking demands a genuine investment in others. Instead of concentrating on what you can gain, prioritize how you can support, contribute to, or learn from the other person.
- **Build Trust:** Trust forms the bedrock of any successful network. Be authentic, honor your commitments, and respect confidentiality. Relationships grounded in trust are far more valuable than fleeting, transactional connections.

2. BE A RESOURCE TO OTHERS

- **Offer Value:** Networking thrives on reciprocity. Share insights, provide introductions, or support others in their endeavors. Your willingness to help fosters goodwill and establishes you as a supportive and reliable presence in your network.
- **Listen and Engage:** Active listening is an essential networking skill. Take the time to understand others' goals, challenges, and needs. Showing genuine interest in their journeys enables you to forge deeper, more meaningful connections.

3. PRIORITIZE QUALITY OVER QUANTITY

- **Be Selective:** While the urge to connect with as many people as possible is understandable, a high-quality network is more impactful than a large one. Seek out individuals who align with your professional values, aspirations, and areas of interest.
- **Nurture Existing Relationships:** Don't neglect the connections you already have. Strengthen these relationships by staying in touch, offering support, and fostering long-term bonds. Often, deep and enduring relationships prove more valuable than new, superficial ones.

4. FOSTER MUTUAL GROWTH AND SUCCESS

- **Encourage Collaboration:** Networking should create opportunities for shared growth. Look for ways to collaborate on projects, share resources, or pursue common goals. When you position yourself as an ally in others' success, they are more likely to reciprocate.
- **Celebrate** Achievements: Recognize and celebrate the accomplishments of your connections. Whether it's a promotion, new role, or project milestone, showing genuine support strengthens the relationship and reinforces your reputation as a positive and encouraging presence.

5. COMMIT TO LONG-TERM RELATIONSHIP BUILDING

- **Be Consistent:** Networking is not a one-time effort but an ongoing process. Regular check-ins, meaningful engagement, and timely follow-ups keep connections vibrant and relevant.
- **Evolve Your Network:** As your career progresses, your network should grow and adapt with you. Periodically evaluate your connections to ensure they align with your current goals and priorities, and remain open to forming new relationships that reflect your evolving interests.

By focusing on these principles, you can cultivate a network that not only supports your professional growth but also fosters meaningful, lasting relationships. Effective networking is not just about collecting contacts—it's about building connections that matter.

NETWORKING AS A FOUNDATION FOR INFLUENCE AND LEADERSHIP

For executives, networking extends far beyond traditional career advancement. A well-cultivated network serves as the cornerstone for establishing influence, driving meaningful change, and fostering innovation within an industry. By nurturing relationships rooted in trust, reciprocity, and shared values, executives can expand their reach, inspire others, and leave a lasting impact. Below, we explore how adopting a strategic approach to networking can amplify leadership and unlock opportunities for both personal and organizational growth.

POSITION YOURSELF AS A THOUGHT LEADER

A strong network not only connects you to influential peers but also amplifies your voice, enabling you to share insights, perspectives, and innovations with a wider audience. A broad-reaching network provides a platform for demonstrating thought leadership through industry discussions, speaking engagements, and digital content. Your network acts as a natural amplifier, disseminating your ideas within their circles and reinforcing your reputation as a leader with valuable insights.

This amplification can increase your influence, attract followers, and establish you as a trusted authority in your field. For example, consistently sharing insights on emerging trends or innovative practices builds credibility. Over time, your network will turn to you for guidance on industry matters, strengthening your personal brand and elevating your standing as a thought leader who contributes meaningfully to your profession.

DRIVE INDUSTRY CHANGE

Executives with robust networks are uniquely equipped to advocate for and implement change within their industries. A well-connected network grants access to diverse perspectives, resources, and expertise, enabling leaders to build momentum around new ideas or initiatives. Whether you are championing diversity, advancing technological innovation, or promoting ethical practices, a strong network allows you to rally peers, mobilize support, and form coalitions of like-minded leaders.

This capacity to unite people and drive industry change is a powerful asset. Well-connected leaders can influence regulatory developments, set new standards, or promote sustainable practices. By harnessing the collective strength of a network, you enhance your ability to create meaningful, large-scale impact and propel your industry forward.

STRENGTHEN ORGANIZATIONAL SUCCESS

Networking offers significant benefits not only for personal growth but also for organizational success. Leveraging your network can infuse your company with fresh ideas, strategic partnerships, and talent, strengthening its competitive edge. Connections within your network can lead to valuable collaborations, new clients, or reliable suppliers, opening doors to opportunities that drive growth and innovation.

Additionally, a strong network is a critical resource for recruitment. It enables you to attract top-tier talent, especially individuals who align with your organization's values and goals, fostering a cohesive and ambitious workplace culture.

By staying attuned to industry trends and insights through your network, you bring back actionable knowledge that informs strategic decisions, improves operations, and drives innovation within your organization. In this way, networking not only reinforces your personal brand but also directly contributes to the resilience, adaptability, and success of your company.

FINAL THOUGHTS ON NETWORKING FOR EXECUTIVES

Networking is not just an activity—it is a strategic, integral component of executive success. By investing in meaningful connections and prioritizing relationship-building over transactional exchanges, you create a network that acts as a catalyst for growth, innovation, and resilience. Effective networking equips you to adapt to change, seize new opportunities, and build a community of trusted allies who can support your journey—and whom you can support in return.

Embrace networking as a lifelong practice, consistently nurturing relationships that enrich your career and leadership. With a well-developed network, you amplify your influence and position yourself to lead with purpose, vision, and impact across your industry.

2. STRATEGIES FOR IN-PERSON NETWORKING

In-person networking is invaluable for building deep, trust-based connections. Executives who excel in this area often leave a lasting impression and establish genuine rapport that digital interactions alone cannot replicate.

ATTEND INDUSTRY EVENTS AND CONFERENCES

Attending industry events and conferences is one of the most effective ways for executives to expand their networks, gain insights, and establish themselves as thought leaders. These events bring together leaders, experts, and potential collaborators, creating a high-value environment for forging meaningful connections within your field. Here's why participating in these gatherings matters and strategies to maximize their benefits.

WHY IT MATTERS

Industry events and conferences offer direct access to influential players in your sector. Whether your goal is to meet potential collaborators, explore emerging trends, or boost your visibility, these gatherings provide an unparalleled platform. By actively engaging, you not only demonstrate your interest and commitment but also position yourself alongside other thought leaders, opening doors to partnerships, speaking engagements, and opportunities for professional growth.

Furthermore, conferences showcase the latest industry developments, providing a firsthand view of innovations and strategies that can inform your leadership and organizational decisions. This knowledge not only keeps you ahead of the curve but also equips you to make informed, strategic moves within your industry.

STRATEGIES FOR SUCCESS

To get the most out of conferences and industry events, adopt a proactive approach focused on preparation, engagement, and strategic networking.

1. PREPARE AHEAD

Research the event agenda and speakers in advance to approach the gathering with a clear plan. Identify key sessions, panels, or workshops that align with your goals and pinpoint individuals you'd like to connect with. Make a list of attendees or speakers whose expertise aligns with your interests, and prepare thoughtful questions or conversation starters.

For instance, if a speaker specializes in an area you're exploring, frame questions that showcase your knowledge and curiosity about their perspective. This level of preparation ensures you approach conversations with confidence and leave a positive impression on the people you meet.

2. ACTIVELY ENGAGE IN SESSIONS

Participation during sessions highlights your engagement and commitment to the subject matter. Merely attending panels or workshops isn't enough—make the most of Q&A opportunities or group discussions to interact meaningfully.

Asking insightful questions not only contributes to the dialogue but also increases your visibility among attendees and panelists. Engaging in this manner positions you as a thoughtful and involved participant, potentially sparking connections with others who share your interests or are impressed by your contributions.

3. LEVERAGE BREAKS FOR NETWORKING

Breaks between sessions are prime opportunities for informal networking. Use these moments to introduce yourself to fellow attendees, join group discussions, or approach speakers with follow-up questions.

Start conversations with shared experiences from the event rather than diving straight into business topics. This approach often leads to relaxed, authentic exchanges that naturally transition into professional discussions. These brief, informal interactions can serve as the foundation for deeper connections and future collaborations.

By attending industry events and conferences with a strategic mindset, you can create valuable networking opportunities, deepen your industry knowledge, and enhance your visibility as a committed leader. Preparing ahead, actively participating in sessions, and utilizing informal networking moments enable you to leave a lasting impression and form connections that support your long-term professional goals.

As you build your presence at these events, you reinforce your personal brand as a proactive, engaged executive, establishing a platform for lasting influence within your industry.

LEVERAGE LOCAL NETWORKING EVENTS AND MEETUPS

Local networking events and meetups provide executives with unique opportunities to cultivate lasting relationships within their communities. Unlike large conferences or one-time industry events, these gatherings allow for repeated interactions with the same professionals, fostering deeper connections and creating a supportive, accessible network. Below, we explore why local networking matters and share strategies to help you make the most of these opportunities.

WHY IT MATTERS

Attending local networking events enables you to connect with peers, mentors, and potential collaborators nearby, offering the chance to nurture relationships over time. These repeated interactions build trust, deepen mutual understanding, and pave the way for easier collaboration on projects or the exchange of advice. Additionally, a robust local network can provide invaluable insights into regional trends, access to community resources, and opportunities to form partnerships that might not be as readily available through virtual platforms or larger national events.

STRATEGIES FOR BUILDING A LOCAL NETWORK

To maximize the benefits of local networking, adopt a proactive approach by seeking relevant events, joining established organizations, and even hosting your own gatherings that align with your professional goals.

SEEK OUT INDUSTRY-SPECIFIC MEETUPS

Many cities host regular meetups tailored to specific industries or roles, such as technology, finance, or executive leadership. These gatherings often attract like-minded professionals, creating an ideal environment to connect with individuals who share similar interests and goals. Use platforms like Meetup.com, Eventbrite, or LinkedIn groups to discover events that align with your expertise. For instance, if you work in technology, consider attending local tech meetups, product management forums, or innovation workshops. By participating consistently, you become a familiar face within the community, making it easier to form meaningful and lasting connections.

GET INVOLVED IN PROFESSIONAL ORGANIZATIONS

Joining local chapters of industry associations, chambers of commerce, or executive networking groups provides structured opportunities for regular engagement. These organizations frequently host events, roundtables, and panel discussions that bring together professionals dedicated to advancing in their respective fields. In addition to networking, they offer professional development resources, mentorship opportunities, and leadership roles that can boost your visibility within the community. Active involvement in such groups demonstrates your commitment to the field, enhances your credibility, and broadens your local influence.

HOST YOUR OWN EVENTS

If you're looking to create a tailored networking experience, consider organizing your own meetups, workshops, or small gatherings. Hosting events allows you to bring together professionals with shared goals or expertise, fostering meaningful discussions and building a community aligned with your interests. Examples include monthly coffee meetups, quarterly lunch-and-learns, or workshops focused on relevant industry topics. By taking on the role of host, you position yourself as a connector and leader within the community, while also shaping the agenda to reflect your professional values. Over time, this can help you cultivate a loyal network of professionals who value your insights and leadership.

Actively participating in local networking events and meetups enables you to develop a close-knit community of professionals who provide support, share valuable insights, and collaborate on opportunities. By seeking out industry-specific gatherings, joining professional organizations, and hosting your own events, you can establish yourself as a visible, well-connected figure in your local professional landscape. These regular interactions not only strengthen relationships and foster trust but also build a foundation of influence that can significantly enhance your executive brand and professional impact.

NETWORKING AT COMPANY EVENTS AND CROSS-DEPARTMENTAL MEETINGS

Building a strong internal network is a powerful way to enhance collaboration, gain broader insights into organizational goals, and cultivate career-advancing relationships. By connecting with colleagues across departments, you can expand your influence, uncover valuable opportunities for professional growth, and potentially identify mentors or advocates to support your career journey. Here's why fostering an internal network matters and strategies to help you make the most of these opportunities.

WHY IT MATTERS

A robust internal network promotes collaboration and breaks down departmental silos, enabling more effective teamwork on cross-departmental projects. Developing relationships within your organization deepens your understanding of how different teams operate and increases your visibility among leaders and potential mentors. These connections can unlock collaborative projects and learning opportunities, enriching your professional development while aligning you with the company's broader vision.

STRATEGIES FOR EFFECTIVE INTERNAL NETWORKING

To cultivate a productive and supportive network, take advantage of cross-departmental meetings, company-wide initiatives, and opportunities to engage with colleagues from various teams.

1. ATTEND CROSS-FUNCTIONAL MEETINGS

Cross-functional meetings provide a unique opportunity to interact with leaders and team members from other departments, offering valuable insights into company-wide initiatives and priorities. Participate actively in these meetings to better understand the goals, challenges, and contributions of various teams. Use these interactions to connect with colleagues outside your immediate circle, demonstrating genuine interest in their work.

For instance, if your company is launching a new product, attending a meeting with the marketing, product development, and customer support teams can provide a holistic understanding of the initiative. These interactions can help you see the big picture, appreciate diverse perspectives, and identify areas for potential collaboration.

2. JOIN COMPANY INITIATIVES

Engaging in company-wide programs such as diversity and inclusion initiatives, volunteer projects, or innovation committees allows you to meet colleagues from different departments and levels of seniority. These initiatives, often rooted in shared values and goals, foster open communication and camaraderie.

By actively participating, you showcase your commitment to the company's mission and enhance your reputation as a values-driven professional. Additionally, involvement in these programs can provide exposure to senior leaders and decision-makers, increasing the likelihood of mentorship opportunities or career advancement.

3. EXPRESS INTEREST IN OTHER DEPARTMENTS

Demonstrating curiosity about the work being done in other departments is an excellent way to broaden your network and uncover new learning opportunities. Reach out to colleagues in different teams to learn about their roles and responsibilities. Showing genuine interest can lead to meaningful connections, collaborative projects, and mentorship opportunities with individuals whose expertise complements your own.

For example, if you work in finance, engaging with the sales team to understand their challenges could provide valuable insights that improve cross-departmental workflows. This curiosity not only enhances your understanding of the organization but also highlights your openness to collaboration and continuous learning.

By effectively networking within your organization, you build relationships that foster collaboration, support career development, and contribute to a positive workplace culture. Attending cross-functional meetings, participating in company initiatives, and expressing interest in other departments can position you as a well-connected leader who understands and supports broader organizational goals. A strong internal network enhances your visibility and influence, positioning you as a proactive, inclusive leader who values teamwork and continuous growth.

3. STRATEGIES FOR DIGITAL NETWORKING

Digital networking enables professionals to expand their reach beyond geographical boundaries, fostering connections with individuals across the globe. For executives, effective online networking requires consistent engagement, intentional interactions, and an ongoing commitment to building relationships.

LINKEDIN FOR NETWORKING

LinkedIn stands as the premier platform for professional networking, empowering executives and leaders to connect with a global community of peers, mentors, and industry influencers. Beyond establishing connections, it's a powerful tool for cultivating meaningful relationships, showcasing expertise, and staying informed about industry trends. By leveraging LinkedIn strategically, you can amplify your influence, enhance your executive brand, and stay ahead of industry developments.

WHY IT MATTERS

With over 700 million professionals worldwide, LinkedIn offers unparalleled access to experts, leaders, and influencers across diverse industries. For executives, it serves as a digital hub for relationship-building, knowledge sharing, and trend tracking.

The platform breaks geographical barriers, enabling you to connect with professionals who align with your interests, values, or goals. Active engagement fosters relationships that not only support career growth but also create collaborative opportunities and establish your presence as a thought leader in your field.

STRATEGIES FOR EFFECTIVE NETWORKING ON LINKEDIN

To maximize LinkedIn's networking potential, approach every interaction with purpose and thoughtfulness. From sending personalized connection requests to actively engaging with content, here are four key strategies for building a robust professional network on LinkedIn:

SEND PERSONALIZED CONNECTION REQUESTS

Avoid sending generic connection requests. Instead, personalize your message by explaining why you're reaching out. Mention mutual connections, shared interests, or a recent post they shared that resonated with you. Personalized messages demonstrate respect for the recipient's time and convey genuine interest.

For example, if you met someone at a conference, reference the event and highlight a specific takeaway from your conversation. This thoughtful approach not only increases the likelihood of a positive response but also lays the groundwork for a meaningful connection.

ENGAGE WITH POSTS AND ARTICLES

Building a strong network requires more than simply adding connections—active engagement is essential. Support your connections by liking, commenting on, or sharing their posts and articles. Meaningful interactions, such as thoughtful comments or insightful questions, demonstrate genuine interest and encourage deeper conversations.

Consistent engagement helps you stay visible within your network and develop a reputation as a supportive and engaged professional. Over time, these interactions strengthen relationships and enhance your presence on the platform.

JOIN AND PARTICIPATE IN LINKEDIN GROUPS

LinkedIn Groups offer focused spaces to connect with professionals who share your interests or expertise. Join groups relevant to your field, and actively participate in discussions by sharing insights, asking questions, or offering resources.

Contributing to group discussions not only helps you build connections but also positions you as a knowledgeable and engaged professional. By establishing yourself as a valuable member of these communities, you can organically attract new connections and reinforce your credibility as a thought leader.

FOLLOW UP AFTER IN-PERSON MEETINGS

After meeting someone at an event, prioritize sending a LinkedIn connection request. Personalize your message by referencing the event and any topics you discussed. For instance, if you talked about an industry trend at a conference, mention it in your message and suggest continuing the conversation online.

Following up reinforces your interest in maintaining the relationship and helps the other person remember the context of your meeting, making future interactions more meaningful.

By actively engaging, sending personalized connection requests, participating in groups, and following up with contacts, you can build a strong and supportive professional network on LinkedIn. This thoughtful approach fosters connections that go beyond surface-level interactions, strengthening your personal brand, expanding your influence, and positioning you as an engaged, insightful leader in your industry.

With LinkedIn's global reach, you can cultivate a dynamic network that not only supports your career aspirations but also enhances your visibility and credibility as a trusted executive.

TWITTER AND INDUSTRY FORUMS

- **Why It Matters**: Twitter is a valuable platform for industry news and quick updates, while industry-specific forums (like Reddit, StackExchange, or dedicated professional forums) allow for deeper discussions on niche topics.
- **Strategies**:
- **Engage in Hashtag Discussions**: Use hashtags relevant to your industry to join conversations, share insights, and connect with professionals discussing similar topics.
- **Share Valuable Content**: Regularly post links to insightful articles, news updates, or your commentary on industry trends.
- **Participate in Industry Twitter Chats**: Many industries host regular Twitter chats on specific topics. These events can be a great way to meet professionals with similar interests and engage in real-time discussions.

VIRTUAL CONFERENCES AND WEBINARS

- **Why It Matters**: Virtual events have become a convenient way to network with industry professionals and thought leaders without traveling.
- **Strategies**:
- **Introduce Yourself in Chat**: Many virtual conferences and webinars have chat features. Introduce yourself with a brief statement about your role and interest in the topic.
- **Follow Up with Speakers and Attendees**: After the event, connect with speakers or fellow attendees on LinkedIn, mentioning the event and any shared interests.

- **Participate Actively in Q&A**: Ask thoughtful questions during Q&A sessions to stand out and establish yourself as an engaged, informed participant.

4. BUILDING AND MAINTAINING MEANINGFUL CONNECTIONS

Building a network is the first step; nurturing and maintaining connections over time is essential for long-term relationships. Here are effective strategies to ensure your network remains active and mutually beneficial.

FOLLOW UP AND STAY IN TOUCH

- **Why It Matters**: Regular follow-ups keep relationships warm and ensure connections remember you.
- **Strategies**:
- **Send a Thank-You Message**: After meeting someone new, send a thank-you message expressing your appreciation for the conversation and interest in staying in touch.
- **Schedule Periodic Check-Ins**: Set reminders to reach out to key connections every few months. A simple message asking how they've been or commenting on recent achievements is often appreciated.
- **Share Useful Content**: Send relevant articles, updates, or opportunities to connections who might benefit. This demonstrates that you're invested in their success.

OFFER VALUE CONSISTENTLY

- **Why It Matters**: Networking is a two-way street, and providing value strengthens your relationships and makes them more reciprocal.
- **Strategies**:
- **Offer Introductions**: If you know two connections who could benefit from meeting each other, offer an introduction. This shows generosity and positions you as a connector.

- **Volunteer Insights or Assistance**: If a connection is working on a project or experiencing a challenge where you have expertise, offer your insights or assistance.
- **Acknowledge and Congratulate Achievements**: Recognize and celebrate the milestones and successes of your network. A quick congratulatory message or comment on their post goes a long way.

LEVERAGE A NETWORKING CRM OR TRACKING SYSTEM

- **Why It Matters**: As your network grows, keeping track of connections and interactions can become challenging. A system helps you manage follow-ups and maintain consistency.
- **Strategies**:
- **Use LinkedIn's Notes and Tags**: LinkedIn offers features that allow you to tag or make notes on connections, helping you remember how you met or topics discussed.
- **Create a Simple CRM or Spreadsheet**: Track details such as contact information, where you met, and the last time you connected. Include follow-up reminders to keep relationships active.
- **Use a Reminder App**: Set reminders on your calendar or in a task management app to reconnect with key contacts regularly.

HOST VIRTUAL OR IN-PERSON MEETUPS

Hosting virtual or in—person meetups is a powerful way to strengthen your professional relationships by creating a space for meaningful, authentic conversations. Organizing events brings people together, allowing you to deepen connections, share insights, and position yourself as a connector within your industry. Hosting regular meetups with your network reinforces your visibility and enhances your influence by facilitating valuable interactions among your contacts. Here's why hosting events matters and some strategies to maximize their impact.

WHY IT MATTERS

Hosting meetups fosters a sense of community, positioning you as a leader who values connection and collaboration. Inviting people from different parts of your network encourages cross-pollination of ideas and expertise, often leading to new insights and opportunities. By creating a welcoming space for discussions, you strengthen existing relationships and allow others to connect with peers who may benefit from knowing each other. Over time, these gatherings help solidify your reputation as a thoughtful, influential figure who brings value to the professional network.

STRATEGIES FOR SUCCESSFUL MEETUPS

To make the most of your hosting efforts, consider organizing meetups that promote engagement, bring together diverse perspectives, and facilitate meaningful dialogue. Here are some effective formats to consider:

Organize Roundtable Discussions

Hosting a roundtable discussion is an excellent way to bring together a small, focused group of executives or industry experts for an in-depth conversation on a specific topic. Select a relevant theme—such as emerging trends, leadership challenges, or industry innovation—and invite participants who can offer diverse perspectives. Roundtables foster open dialogue, allowing attendees to share insights, exchange ideas, and build meaningful connections. As the host, you're not only facilitating a valuable discussion but also creating an environment where your network can engage with one another, further solidifying your role as a connector.

Host a Virtual Coffee Chat

Virtual coffee chats are informal yet effective opportunities to reconnect with your network and stay updated on their recent activities and interests. Schedule these chats regularly, inviting different individuals each time to keep the conversations engaging and varied. These relaxed gatherings provide a low-pressure setting to catch up, exchange updates, and discuss current trends or challenges. By rotating your guest list, you can ensure consistent interaction with a wide range of contacts. This approach is particularly useful for maintaining relationships with individuals who may not be in your immediate circle but remain valuable allies or collaborators in your professional journey.

Arrange an Annual Networking Event

An annual networking event—whether held in person or virtually—offers a structured opportunity to reconnect with people from various stages of your career. Invite a diverse group, including former colleagues, mentors, and current peers, to foster rich interactions. Such an event not only positions you as a proactive networker and connector but also becomes a recurring occasion that your contacts look forward to each year. Consider centering the event around an industry-relevant topic or hosting it as a casual celebration of professional milestones. By creating an inclusive and welcoming atmosphere, you strengthen your network while enabling your attendees to forge new connections.

Whether through roundtable discussions, virtual coffee chats, or annual networking events, hosting gatherings is a powerful way to nurture professional relationships and enhance your role as a connector. These platforms provide your contacts with valuable opportunities to engage, share ideas, and build relationships. Over time, these efforts not only reinforce your reputation as a leader who values meaningful connections but also foster a dynamic, supportive community that drives your own professional growth and impact.

5. OVERCOMING NETWORKING CHALLENGES

Networking does not always come naturally, even for seasoned executives. Here are strategies for overcoming common networking challenges:

- **If You're Introverted**: Focus on quality over quantity. Seek out smaller, more intimate events where you can engage in meaningful, one-on-one conversations.
- **If You're Short on Time**: Use digital networking tools like LinkedIn and Twitter to engage in quick, meaningful interactions. Schedule brief check-ins rather than long meetings.
- **If You're Unsure of Your Networking Goals**: Reflect on your career goals and identify what kind of connections would help you reach them—target events and platforms where those professionals are active.

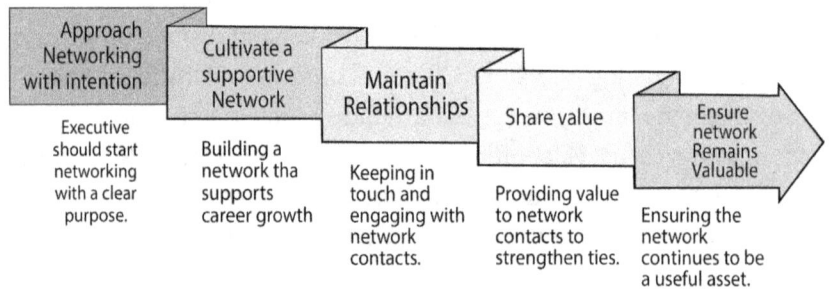

Networking and Relationship-Building for Executives

CONCLUSION

Networking and relationship-building are essential for long-term executive success. By approaching networking with intention—whether in person or online—you can cultivate a powerful, supportive network that elevates your career and enhances your influence in the industry. Maintaining relationships through regular engagement, value-sharing, and consistent follow-ups ensures that your network remains valuable throughout your professional journey. In the next chapter, we'll delve into establishing thought leadership and creating content that enhances your brand.

UNLOCK THE MAGIC—
SCAN, TO LEARN MORE!

THOUGHT LEADERSHIP AND CONTENT CREATION

THE IMPORTANCE OF THOUGHT LEADERSHIP FOR EXECUTIVES

Thought leadership is a transformative way for executives to establish authority, build credibility, and share their unique perspectives with a wide audience. By positioning yourself as a thought leader, you not only enhance your personal brand but also contribute meaningfully to your industry by offering valuable insights, innovative ideas, and actionable guidance. Thought leadership goes beyond merely sharing knowledge—it's about becoming a trusted, go-to source for solutions, direction, and inspiration.

In this chapter, we explore how executives can leverage content creation—through articles, podcasts, webinars, and public speaking—to craft a compelling thought leadership profile. We'll delve into strategies for amplifying your reach and impact through effective content distribution, and we'll examine how AI tools can help create a customized path tailored to your expertise and experiences.

1. ESTABLISHING AUTHORITY THROUGH THOUGHT LEADERSHIP

Thought leadership is not about self-promotion; it's about providing value, fostering insights, and driving meaningful conversations within your field. To establish yourself as an authority in your industry, you must approach thought leadership with intentionality, consistency, and authenticity. Here's how thought leadership can elevate your professional profile:

- **Building Trust and Credibility**: Consistently sharing insights on relevant industry topics demonstrates your expertise and earns the trust of your audience.

- **Expanding Your Influence**: Thought leadership positions you as a key voice in your field, enabling you to shape industry trends and guide critical discussions.
- **Attracting Opportunities**: As a recognized thought leader, you naturally become a preferred candidate for speaking engagements, board positions, consulting roles, and media appearances.

Throught Leadership

Building Trust

Expanding Influence

Attracting Opportunities

Creating Impact

- **Creating Lasting Impact**: Through thought leadership, you can contribute to your industry's collective knowledge base, leaving a legacy that transcends your individual achievements.

2. CONTENT CREATION STRATEGIES FOR THOUGHT LEADERSHIP

Creating valuable, consistent content is central to thought leadership. Each type of content—written, audio, video, or in-person presentation—offers unique opportunities to engage with your audience and establish authority.

ARTICLES AND BLOG POSTS

Writing articles or blog posts is one of the most effective ways to communicate your insights, share lessons learned, and showcase expertise in specific areas.

- **Why It Matters**: Articles provide in-depth analysis of topics relevant to your industry, allowing you to demonstrate expertise and thoughtfulness. Publishing regularly also keeps your name at the forefront of your mind.
- **Best Practices**:
- **Identify Key Topics**: Choose topics that align with your unique value proposition (UVP) and your industry's pressing challenges. Content should reflect your knowledge and experience in areas where you bring unique insights.
- **Use Data and Case Studies**: Support your insights with data, case studies, or examples from your own experience to make your articles credible and practical.
- **Publish on Reputable Platforms**: Consider publishing on platforms like LinkedIn, Medium, or industry-specific websites to reach a broader audience. Pitch guest articles to publications like Forbes, Inc Magazine, Harvard Business Review, or industry journals for added credibility.

AUDIO AND VIDEO PODCASTING: EXPANDING THOUGHT LEADERSHIP THROUGH CONVERSATIONS

Podcasting, in audio and video, helps executives build authority, connect with audiences, and showcase expertise. It enables conversational discussions on complex topics, offering insights and value. Being a guest or hosting your own podcast amplifies reach, builds credibility, and strengthens connections with busy professionals and industry peers.

WHY PODCASTING MATTERS FOR EXECUTIVES

Video and audio content humanizes your brand, creating a personal, engaging platform. Podcasts, ideal for busy professionals, deliver expert insights on-demand. Hosting or featuring on podcasts builds thought leadership, fosters deep topic exploration, and connects you with industry audiences, enhancing your brand's reach and credibility in a conversational format.

GETTING FEATURED ON ESTABLISHED PODCASTS

One of the most effective ways to build authority and grow your audience is by guesting on popular podcasts, particularly those that are industry-specific or centered around leadership. Established podcasts come with loyal audiences, and being featured enables you to tap into that platform, reaching listeners who trust the host and are eager to gain insights from expert guests.

STEPS TO GET FEATURED ON OTHER PODCASTS

Research Relevant Podcasts: Begin by identifying podcasts that align with your industry or focus on themes such as leadership, innovation, or topics related to your expertise. Platforms like Apple Podcasts, Spotify, and niche industry forums are great tools to help you discover suitable shows.

Craft a Compelling Pitch: Personalize your pitch for each podcast to demonstrate why you're an ideal guest. Highlight your unique insights, recent accomplishments, or perspectives that would resonate with their audience. Make it clear what value you can add to the show.

Prepare for the Interview: Once you're invited, approach the interview as a strategic opportunity to showcase your knowledge. Listen to past episodes to understand the host's style and the interests of their audience. Prepare key talking points or stories that align with the podcast's theme and will engage listeners.

Engage and Promote: After the episode airs, share it with your network, tagging the podcast and the host to express your gratitude and encourage engagement. Actively promoting your guest appearance not only shows appreciation but also boosts your visibility within your network.

Follow-up: Keep the relationship with the host alive after the episode. Send a thank-you note for the opportunity, and stay in touch for potential future collaborations or guest appearances.

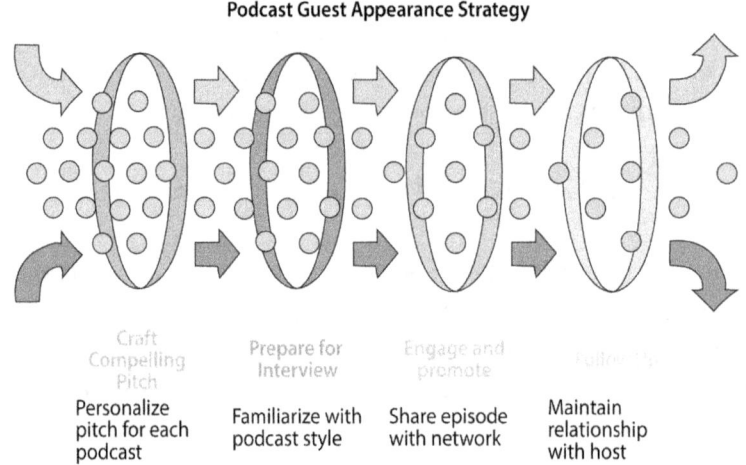

BENEFITS OF GUEST-APPEARING ON PODCASTS

- **Enhanced Credibility**: Being invited as a guest on reputable podcasts demonstrates that others recognize your expertise, reinforcing your authority in your field.
- **Audience Expansion**: You gain exposure to a broader audience, many of whom may not have otherwise encountered your work.
- **Networking**: Podcast hosts are often influential within their networks. Building relationships with them can open doors to other speaking engagements or industry opportunities.
- **SEO and Discoverability**: Many podcasts also publish transcripts or blog posts that link back to your website or profile, enhancing your search engine optimization (SEO) and making it easier for people to find you online.

CREATING YOUR OWN PODCAST: BUILDING A DIRECT CHANNEL TO YOUR AUDIENCE

Launching your own podcast is a powerful way to amplify your thought leadership and create a unique, engaging platform to connect with your audience. Hosting a podcast puts you in control of your content, allowing you to build a narrative that aligns with your professional goals and brand values. Not only does a podcast provide a regular touchpoint with your listeners, but it also opens up opportunities for networking and collaboration with other industry leaders. Here's why starting a podcast matters for your thought leadership and how it can enhance your executive brand.

CONTENT CONTROL

One of the greatest benefits of hosting your own podcast is the ability to choose topics that best showcase your expertise and align with your career objectives. You control the narrative, selecting themes, discussions, and insights that highlight your unique perspectives. This freedom allows you to share your knowledge on issues that matter to you, whether it's innovation, leadership, or industry trends. By consistently delivering valuable insights, you position yourself as a reliable source of knowledge, reinforcing your reputation as a thought leader. The ability to control your content also ensures that each episode aligns with your long-term goals, allowing you to shape how others perceive your expertise.

AUDIENCE ENGAGEMENT

Podcasts offer a personal way to engage, building trust and loyalty through regular episodes. They create a sense of connection, making complex topics relatable. By sharing stories and insights conversationally, podcasts foster intimacy and build a loyal audience, enhancing your influence as a thought leader.

NETWORKING OPPORTUNITIES

Inviting guests to your podcast gives you the opportunity to connect with industry leaders, experts, and potential collaborators. By featuring guests whose expertise complements or contrasts with your own, you create rich, diverse conversations that add value to your audience. Each guest also brings their own network of followers, potentially expanding your reach to new audiences. These interactions can lead to future collaborations, partnerships, or even new client relationships. Hosting a podcast positions you as both a peer and a connector, strengthening your professional relationships and solidifying your reputation as an industry influencer.

BRAND CONSISTENCY

Every podcast episode serves as a lasting piece of content that reinforces your brand. From the topics you choose to the tone of each conversation, every element reflects your professional values, expertise, and personality. Maintaining a consistent release schedule and ensuring high-quality production builds credibility and strengthens your presence as a thought leader. Consistent messaging, aligned with your brand values, helps listeners understand what you stand for and builds a cohesive image of your expertise. Over time, this consistency reinforces your authority, making your podcast a trusted resource for your audience.

Starting your own podcast provides a dynamic platform to expand your influence, engage with your audience, and strengthen your thought leadership. A podcast becomes a cornerstone of your executive brand through content control, regular audience interaction, strategic guest invitations, and consistent branding. It showcases your expertise and creates a community of engaged listeners and connections, amplifying your impact and positioning you as a leading voice in your industry.

BEST PRACTICES FOR LAUNCHING AND RUNNING A SUCCESSFUL PODCAST

Choose a Clear and Focused Theme

- **Identify Your Niche**: Select a theme that reflects your expertise and adds value to your target audience. Your theme should address relevant industry challenges, trends, or innovations. Examples include "Navigating Digital Transformation in Finance" or "Leadership Lessons from the C-Suite."
- **Define Your Audience**: Know who you're trying to reach. Are you speaking to industry peers, potential clients, or emerging professionals? Tailoring content to a specific audience helps create more impactful episodes.

Plan and Structure Each Episode

- **Consistent Format**: Establish a format for each episode, whether a solo talk, interview, or panel discussion. Consistency helps your audience know what to expect.

- **Prepare Key Points**: Outline key discussion points, questions for guests, or segments within each episode. Structured content is more engaging and keeps listeners invested.
- **Limit Episode Length:** Keep episodes manageable (20-40 minutes is typical) to hold your audience's attention, especially if they're listening during a commute or between meetings.

Invest in Quality Equipment

- **Microphone**: A high-quality microphone is essential for clear audio. Consider models like the **Blue Yeti** or **Audio-Technica AT2020** for professional sound.
- **Recording Software:** Tools like **Audacity** (free) or **Adobe Audition** provide reliable recording and editing capabilities.
- **Video Option**: Recording video along with audio can add a visual element, allowing you to repurpose content for YouTube or social media clips.

Feature High-Value Guests

- **Invite Industry Leaders and Influencers**: Bring guests with unique insights strong professional reputations, or align with your target audience's interests.
- **Leverage Cross-Promotion**: When guests share episodes with their networks, it extends your reach and introduces your podcast to new listeners.
- **Engage in Meaningful Conversations**: Prepare thoughtful, open-ended questions encouraging guests to share stories, advice, and insights, making the conversation valuable for your audience.

Consistency in Publishing

- **Establish a Regular Schedule**: Whether weekly, bi-weekly, or monthly, publishing on a consistent schedule builds anticipation and loyalty among listeners.
- **Plan Content in Batches**: Recording multiple episodes in advance can ensure a steady flow of content, even during busy periods.

Promote Across Multiple Platforms

- **Social Media**: Share each episode on LinkedIn, Twitter, and Instagram, with brief descriptions or highlights to attract listeners.
- **Cross-Promote with Your Guests**: Encourage guests to share their episodes, expanding your reach to their network.

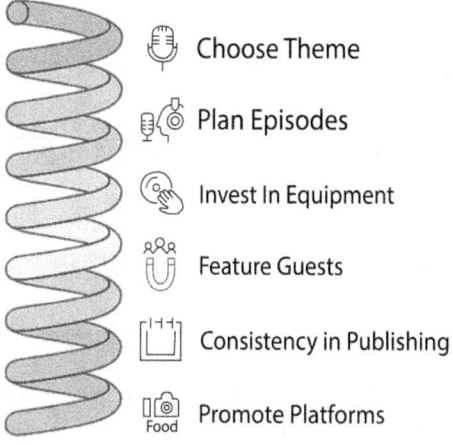

- **Email Newsletter**: Include new episodes in your newsletter or dedicated email campaigns to keep your subscriber base updated.

REPURPOSING PODCAST CONTENT FOR EXTENDED REACH

To maximize the impact of each podcast episode, repurpose the content across different formats and platforms:

- **Social Media Clips**: Create short audio or video snippets from each episode to share as "highlights" on LinkedIn, Twitter, Instagram, or TikTok.
- **Blog Summaries or Transcripts**: Publish a summary or transcript of each episode on your website to enhance discoverability and provide an alternative format for those who prefer reading.
- **YouTube Videos**: If you record video along with audio, post full episodes or clips on YouTube to reach a larger audience and increase engagement.

TOOLS TO ENHANCE YOUR PODCASTING EXPERIENCE

A few tools can help streamline your podcasting process and ensure quality output:

- **Descript**: This tool allows for easy audio editing and transcription, making it simpler to create snippets, add captions, or repurpose content.
- **Headliner**: Use this tool to create audiograms and visually engaging snippets with captions for social media. It is ideal for promoting podcast highlights.
- **Buzzsprout or Anchor**: These podcast hosting platforms make it easy to distribute episodes to all major platforms (Apple Podcasts, Spotify, Google Podcasts) and offer analytics to track listener engagement.
- **Calendly**: Calendly integrates with calendar systems for scheduling interviews with guests, reducing the back-and-forth of finding a time to record.

Podcasting is a powerful platform for executives looking to establish and maintain thought leadership. Whether appearing as a guest on established shows or hosting your own podcast, you can reach a wide audience, provide value, and build credibility in your industry. With the right approach, podcasting enables you to engage in meaningful conversations, expand your network, and solidify your brand as a trusted voice in your field.

WEBINARS AND VIDEO CONTENT: LEVERAGING VISUAL ENGAGEMENT FOR THOUGHT LEADERSHIP

Webinars and videos are powerful tools for thought leadership, offering accessible insights, real-time engagement, and personal connections. They foster trust, enable storytelling, and allow instant audience interaction, creating opportunities to engage deeply and effectively beyond written content.

WHY WEBINARS AND VIDEO CONTENT MATTER FOR EXECUTIVES

In an increasingly digital world, video content is more engaging and memorable than text alone. Webinars and videos allow you to reach a broad audience and provide a platform for interactive learning and immediate feedback. Here's why they're essential for thought leadership:

- **Direct Audience Interaction**: Webinars and live videos allow for real-time interaction, making it easier to build a connection, answer specific questions, and clarify complex ideas.
- **Depth of Communication**: Video content allows you to dive deeply into nuanced topics, presenting visual aids, charts, and demonstrations that enhance understanding.
- **Building Trust and Relatability**: Seeing and hearing you speak helps audiences connect with you on a personal level, reinforcing your credibility and authenticity.

- **Long-Term Content Value:** Recorded webinars and videos can be repurposed into various formats, extending their reach and lifespan beyond the initial live event.

BEST PRACTICES FOR CREATING EFFECTIVE WEBINARS AND VIDEO CONTENT

To maximize the impact of webinars and video content, it's crucial to focus on high-impact topics, engage with your audience through interactive elements, and repurpose content for maximum reach.

1. FOCUS ON HIGH-IMPACT TOPICS

- **Choose Timely, Relevant Topics:** Select topics that resonate with current trends, pain points, or emerging challenges within your industry. High-impact topics attract more viewers and position you as a proactive leader addressing real issues.
- **Align Topics with Your Expertise:** Your content should reflect your unique value proposition (UVP) and showcase your expertise in areas relevant to your audience. Focusing on topics within your domain helps reinforce your credibility.
- **Solve Specific Problems:** Webinars that promise solutions to common industry problems or offer step-by-step guidance are highly valued by audiences. Structure the content around practical takeaways and actionable insights.

Example: An executive specializing in digital marketing might host a webinar on "Maximizing ROI in a Post-Cookie World," addressing recent changes in data privacy and offering practical strategies.

2. STRUCTURE YOUR WEBINAR OR VIDEO WITH ENGAGING VISUALS AND CLEAR SECTIONS

- **Organize Content into Sections**: Break down your content into clear, easily digestible segments. This helps keep the audience's attention and provides natural transition points.
- **Use Visual Aids and Demonstrations**: Incorporate slides, graphics, and live demonstrations where appropriate. Visual aids make complex information more understandable and memorable.
- **Include Key Takeaways**: Summarize each segment with key takeaways or action points. This helps reinforce important information and gives viewers practical insights to implement.

Example: In a webinar on data analytics, an executive might include visuals showing data trends, followed by actionable steps for implementing data-driven strategies. Each section could end with a slide highlighting the main points.

3. INCLUDE INTERACTIVE ELEMENTS

- **Live Q&A Sessions**: Schedule time for Q&A either during or after the main presentation. Live Q&A sessions provide valuable audience insights and allow you to address specific questions, fostering engagement.
- **Polls and Surveys**: Use polls to gauge audience opinions, test knowledge, or encourage participation. This interaction keeps the session dynamic and allows you to adjust the content based on responses.
- **Breakout Rooms**: If your webinar platform supports breakout rooms, use them for smaller group discussions or deeper dives into subtopics. Breakout rooms allow participants to engage with each other, creating a more collaborative experience.
- **Chat Features**: Encourage participants to share thoughts or ask questions via chat. Assign a moderator to monitor the chat and bring relevant questions or comments to your attention during the session.

Example: In a webinar on leadership development, you might start with a poll asking attendees about their biggest leadership challenges. During the Q&A, prioritize addressing the challenges that received the most responses, making the session more relevant to the audience's needs.

4. REPURPOSE VIDEO CONTENT FOR EXTENDED REACH

One of the greatest advantages of video and webinar content is its versatility. After the live event, you can repurpose the content into various formats to reach new audiences and maximize its impact.

- **Record the Webinar for On-Demand Viewing**: Many attendees may be unable to join the live event, so make the recorded version available for on-demand access. Hosting the recording on your website or YouTube channel increases accessibility and expands its reach.
- **Create Short Video Snippets for Social Media**: Extract key moments or highlights from the webinar and create short, engaging clips for social media. Platforms like LinkedIn, Instagram, and Twitter are ideal for sharing snippets that drive viewers to the full video.
- **Convert Content into Blog Posts or Articles**: Write a summary or detailed article based on the webinar's content, covering the main points and insights shared during the session. This extends your reach to readers and reinforces your thought leadership.
- **Use as Training Material**: Webinars that cover foundational topics or skill-building content can serve as valuable training materials for your team or company, especially for onboarding or professional development.

Example: If you held a 45-minute webinar on "Future Trends in AI for Healthcare," you could:

- Post the full video on YouTube and LinkedIn.
- Create 2-3 short clips (under 1 minute each) with insights on specific trends for social media.
- Write a blog post titled "5 Key Trends from My Recent AI Webinar" and share it on your website and LinkedIn profile.

5. OPTIMIZE VIDEO CONTENT FOR SEO AND DISCOVERABILITY

Search engine optimization (SEO) is o't limited to written content; it also applies to video content. Optimizing video and webinar recordings increases their discoverability, allowing new audiences to find and engage with your content.

- **Use Descriptive Titles and Keywords**: Craft a clear, engaging title with relevant keywords. For example, "How to Implement AI in Retail" is more searchable than a generic title like "AI Webinar."
- **Add Captions and Transcriptions**: Many viewers watch videos on mute, especially on social media. Captions make content accessible to all viewers and improve SEO, as search engines can index the transcription.
- **Write a Detailed Description**: Include a detailed description with relevant keywords for platforms like YouTube. Add timestamps to help viewers navigate the content, especially for longer videos.
- **Include Relevant Tags and Hashtags**: Use tags and hashtags related to the video's topic. This enhances visibility on platforms that rely on hashtags (like Instagram or Twitter) and categorizes your content effectively on YouTube.

Example: For a YouTube video on "Improving Customer Experience with AI," the description might include a summary of key points, links to related resources, and keywords like "customer experience," "artificial intelligence," and "CX strategies."

6. PROMOTE THE WEBINAR OR VIDEO BEFORE, DURING, AND AFTER THE EVENT

Effective promotion ensures maximum attendance and ongoing engagement with your video content.

- **Pre-Event Marketing**: Send invitations via email newsletters, LinkedIn posts, and industry forums. Share the event details with your network and encourage team members to promote it on their channels.
- **Live Engagement**: During the live event, encourage attendees to share their thoughts on social media with a designated hashtag, driving further engagement and visibility.
- **Post-Event Follow-Up**: Follow up with attendees after the event by sharing the recording and any additional resources. Send a thank-you email with links to relevant articles, blog posts, or future webinars.

Example: For a webinar on "Navigating Data Privacy Laws," you could promote it with posts on LinkedIn leading up to the event, asking registrants to share what they're most interested in learning. During the event, prompt attendees to post takeaways using a unique hashtag, and after the event, send an email with the recording and links to related articles.

TOOLS FOR CREATING AND HOSTING WEBINARS AND VIDEO CONTENT

Having the right tools can significantly impact the quality and reach of your webinars and videos.

- **Webinar Platforms: Zoom** and **Webex** are popular choices for hosting live webinars with large audiences. Both platforms offer interactive features like Q&A, polls, and breakout rooms.
- **Video Recording and Editing Tools: Camtasia** is an excellent screen recording and editing tool, ideal for creating tutorial videos. **Adobe Premiere Pro** or **Final Cut Pro** provides advanced editing features for professional-grade video content.
- **Social Media Scheduling: Hootsuite** or **Buffer** can help you schedule and promote webinar content across multiple social media channels, ensuring consistent visibility.
- **Transcription Services: Otter.ai** and **Descript** offer transcription services that are useful for creating captions, summaries, and repurposing content into written formats.

Webinars and video content have become invaluable tools for executives aiming to establish thought leadership and engage with their audiences more effectively. By focusing on relevant, high-impact topics, integrating interactive elements, and repurposing content for multiple platforms, you can significantly extend the reach and impact of each session. Leveraging SEO strategies, promoting content effectively, and using the right tools ensures that your webinars and videos not only connect with the right audience but also help build trust and reinforce your expertise as a leader in your field.

PUBLIC SPEAKING ENGAGEMENTS: AMPLIFYING AUTHORITY THROUGH DIRECT INTERACTION

Public speaking is one of the most powerful ways for executives to build authority, enhance visibility, and engage directly with their target audience. Whether speaking at conferences, industry panels, corporate events, or virtual summits, these engagements provide an unparalleled platform to share insights, establish credibility, and connect with other thought leaders. In today's competitive business environment, public speaking isn't just a way to showcase expertise—it's an opportunity to influence, inspire, and drive conversations that shape industry trends.

WHY PUBLIC SPEAKING MATTERS FOR EXECUTIVES

Public speaking engagements have a far-reaching impact that extends beyond the immediate event. Here's why they are crucial for thought leadership:

- **Enhanced Visibility and Authority**: Presenting at respected industry events positions you as a knowledgeable figure in your field. Audiences tend to view speakers as authorities, and being invited to speak signals that you offer valuable insights.
- **Immediate Connection with Your Audience**: Speaking directly to an audience allows for real-time interaction, giving you the chance to gauge reactions, answer questions, and clarify ideas on the spot. This fosters a deeper connection that's difficult to achieve with written content alone.
- **Networking and Influence**: Events often bring together industry leaders, potential collaborators, and decision-makers. Public speaking engagements present a unique opportunity to network and form relationships that can lead to future opportunities.

- **Content Creation Opportunity**: Every speaking engagement can be recorded, summarized, or repurposed for additional content. Sharing clips, key takeaways, or even full recordings on your website and social media channels extends the lifespan of the presentation and allows you to reach a broader audience.

BEST PRACTICES FOR EFFECTIVE PUBLIC SPEAKING

To maximize the impact of your speaking engagements, it's essential to approach each one with a clear strategy and engaging delivery. Here are some best practices to ensure that your message resonates and leaves a lasting impression:

1. CURATE YOUR KEY MESSAGE

- **Focus on a Core Theme**: Identify a central message that reflects your expertise, values, and the needs of your audience. This message should be clear, relevant, and impactful, serving as the backbone of your presentation.
- **Align with Thought Leadership Goals**: Consider how your message reinforces your goals as a thought leader. For instance, if your goal is to establish authority in digital transformation, your presentation could focus on actionable insights or innovations in this area.
- **Tailor Content to the Audience**: Customize your message according to the event and the demographics of your audience. For a general audience, focus on broader concepts. For industry-specific panels, you can delve into technical or niche topics.

Example: An executive specializing in sustainable business practices could center their message around "Building a Profitable, Sustainable Future." This topic aligns with their expertise and attracts audiences interested in eco-friendly innovations and ethical business practices.

2. ENGAGE THROUGH STORYTELLING

- **Use Personal Stories**: Stories from your own career make your presentation relatable and memorable. Share specific experiences—successes, failures, or pivotal moments—that illustrate your message and demonstrate your expertise.
- **Incorporate Case Studies and Examples**: Use case studies or real-world examples that reinforce your message if personal stories aren't available. Highlighting how companies have successfully implemented strategies or overcome challenges adds credibility to your talk.
- **Create a Narrative Arc**: Structure your presentation like a story, with a clear beginning, middle, and end. Start with a compelling introduction, lead into the core insights or lessons, and conclude with actionable takeaways that inspire the audience.

Example: Instead of discussing "leadership" in abstract terms, an executive could share a story of leading a team through a challenging project, detailing the obstacles, decisions made, and the outcome. This approach provides a practical example that audiences can relate to and learn from.

3. LEVERAGE VISUAL AIDS AND ENGAGEMENT TOOLS

- **Use Engaging Visuals**: Slide decks, infographics, and videos can significantly improve comprehension and maintain audience engagement. Use visuals strategically and sparingly, focusing on images or graphs that clarify or reinforce key points.
- **Incorporate Interactive Elements**: Polls, Q&A sessions, or live demonstrations can turn your presentation into an interactive experience, encouraging active participation and increasing audience investment.

- **Simplify Complex Concepts**: For technical or complex topics, consider using analogies, metaphors, or simplified graphics to make your message more accessible to a broader audience.

Example: If presenting data-heavy insights, break down each point with visual aids like bar graphs or infographics. These visuals not only improve understanding but also create a more memorable impact.

4. ENCOURAGE AUDIENCE PARTICIPATION

- **Ask Open-Ended Questions**: Throughout the presentation, ask questions to involve the audience, making them feel part of the conversation. This can also provide useful insights into their perspectives or experiences.
- **Host a Q&A Session**: Toward the end of your talk, offer a Q&A session. This allows the audience to engage directly, ask for clarifications, and deepen their understanding of your message.
- **Encourage Social Media Interaction**: If appropriate, encourage the audience to tweet or post insights, using a specific hashtag to drive online engagement. This increases visibility beyond the room and connects you with your audience online.

Example: For a presentation on digital innovation, you might ask the audience, "What's the biggest digital challenge your company is facing today?" and invite responses. This engages the audience and gives you insights that could be useful for further discussion.

5. RECORD AND REPURPOSE YOUR PRESENTATIONS

- **Obtain Permission to Record**: If the event permits, record your presentation to use it as future content. A high-quality recording is an asset for promoting your brand on digital platforms.
- **Share on Social Media and Your Website**: Post the full recording, or select impactful clips, on your website, LinkedIn, and YouTube.

Short clips can be shared on platforms like Twitter and Instagram to capture attention and drive viewers to the full talk.
- **Repurpose for Blogs, Newsletters, and Articles**: Summarize your talk or expand on key points in a blog post, LinkedIn article, or email newsletter. This allows your message to reach a wider audience, including those who may not have attended the event.

Example: After a presentation on effective leadership, you could create a blog post titled "5 Leadership Lessons from My Recent Talk at [Event Name]." This expands the reach of your message and reinforces your thought leadership.

6. FOLLOW UP AND BUILD RELATIONSHIPS

- **Engage with Attendees Post-Event**: Follow up with attendees, especially those who asked questions or showed particular interest after the event. Send a thank-you message and provide any additional resources you may have discussed.
- **Network with Other Speakers**: Connect with fellow speakers and panelists, as they are often thought leaders or influential figures within your industry. Building relationships with other speakers can lead to future collaborations or invitations to other events.
- **Solicit Feedback**: Seek feedback from event organizers or attendees. Constructive feedback can help you refine your speaking skills and effectively tailor future presentations.

Example: After presenting at a conference, follow up with key attendees via LinkedIn, expressing appreciation for their interest and offering to connect. You might also ask for feedback on the presentation to help improve for future engagements.

USING PUBLIC SPEAKING AS A FOUNDATION FOR FURTHER CONTENT CREATION

Public speaking engagements create a wealth of content opportunities. By repurposing and expanding on your presentations, you can reach a larger audience and solidify your thought leadership:

- **Write an Article or Blog Post**: Transform your presentation into an article summarizing the main points and adding additional context or data.
- **Create a Podcast Episode**: Record a podcast episode based on the talk, delving deeper into the key points or discussing new insights you may have gathered from the audience's questions.
- **Develop a Series of Social Media Posts**: Break down the presentation into bite-sized insights, tips, or quotes that can be shared as posts on LinkedIn, Twitter, and Instagram.

Example: If your presentation covered "Trends in AI and Business," you could write an article titled "Top AI Trends Every Executive Should Know," record a podcast episode expanding on one trend, and share a series of quotes from the talk as individual social media posts.

Public speaking is a powerful tool for executives who want to amplify their authority, expand their influence, and engage with audiences more personally. By carefully crafting your message, engaging through storytelling, and repurposing the content across digital platforms, you can significantly extend the impact of each speaking engagement. Public speaking allows you to make a lasting impression, and with a thoughtful follow-up strategy, it can lead to a network of connections, future collaborations, and a solidified position as a thought leader in your field.

DISTRIBUTION STRATEGIES FOR MAXIMIZING REACH AND IMPACT

Creating content is only part of thought leadership; effectively distributing it to your audience is essential for building a strong presence. Here are some proven strategies for maximizing reach:

LEVERAGE SOCIAL MEDIA PLATFORMS

Each social media platform has unique strengths, so tailor your distribution strategy accordingly.

- **LinkedIn**: LinkedIn is essential for executives. Share articles, comment on trending topics, and engage with connections to increase visibility. Consider LinkedIn's article feature and even start a LinkedIn Newsletter for regular content.
- **Twitter**: Use Twitter to share quick insights, industry news, or promote longer content. Engage with other thought leaders by joining discussions and using relevant hashtags.
- **YouTube**: Upload webinars, interviews, and video content to YouTube. Use YouTube Shorts for quick, engaging content that offers value in less than a minute.

CROSS-PROMOTE CONTENT ON MULTIPLE CHANNELS

Promote content across all your digital platforms to maximize visibility and engagement.

- **Email Newsletters**: Send a monthly or quarterly newsletter summarizing your latest articles, upcoming webinars, or speaking engagements. Encourage subscribers to engage with and share the content.
- **Repurpose Content**: Turn a single article into multiple formats, such as infographics, blog posts, short videos, or social media

posts. Repurposing increases your reach without requiring entirely new content.
- **Collaborate with Influencers and Peers**: Partner with other thought leaders, invite them to co-author articles, or feature them as podcast guests. Cross-promotion helps you tap into each other's networks.

OPTIMIZE FOR SEARCH ENGINES (SEO)

Optimizing content for search engines ensures it's discoverable by those searching for topics related to your expertise.

- **Use Relevant Keywords**: Research and use keywords relevant to your industry and content topic. Tools like Google Keyword Planner or SEMrush can help identify popular keywords.
- **Write SEO-Friendly Headlines**: Titles should be clear, concise, and include relevant keywords to improve searchability.
- **Add Metadata**: For blog posts, YouTube videos, and articles on your website, include meta descriptions and tags that describe the content and improve its search ranking.

USING AI TO ENHANCE THOUGHT LEADERSHIP CONTENT

Artificial intelligence (AI) can be invaluable for executives seeking to build thought leadership efficiently and strategically. AI can analyze your profile details, work history, and previous content to identify the most relevant and impactful topics for you to cover.

CONTENT IDEATION AND TOPIC SUGGESTIONS

AI can analyze your LinkedIn profile, About section, and work history to suggest specific content topics that align with your expertise, strengths, and industry trends.

- **How It Works**: By examining your past roles, accomplishments, and the skills highlighted in your profile, AI tools can recommend topics that match your brand and position you as a thought leader.
- **Practical Application**: AI tools like Jasper, Copy.ai, or even LinkedIn's AI writing assistant can suggest blog titles, article ideas, or video topics based on keywords in your profile. For example, if your profile highlights "digital transformation," AI might suggest topics like "The Role of AI in Modernizing Business Operations" or "Navigating Digital Change in Established Enterprises."

CONTENT DRAFTING AND OPTIMIZATION

AI can help draft articles, summaries, or social media posts based on topics you provide, saving time while maintaining quality.

- **How It Works**: With input on your intended message and audience, AI content tools can create first drafts or summaries of articles, posts, or podcast scripts.
- **Practical Application**: Use AI tools like ChatGPT to draft initial versions of articles or social media posts, which you can refine to add your unique voice. These tools can also provide summaries for complex topics, making it easier to explain technical subjects in an accessible way.

AUDIENCE INSIGHTS AND ANALYTICS

AI can provide valuable insights into your audience's preferences, helping you tailor content to their interests and maximize engagement.

- **How It Works**: AI-powered analytics tools (like Google Analytics or LinkedIn Analytics) provide insights into which topics resonate most with your audience, engagement levels, and preferred platforms.
- **Practical Application**: Review analytics data to understand which content types and topics drive engagement most. Adjust your

strategy to prioritize content formats or subjects that align with your audience's interests.

BUILDING A CONSISTENT THOUGHT LEADERSHIP STRATEGY

Establishing yourself as a thought leader is an ongoing process that requires consistency, authenticity, and adaptability.

- **Develop a Content Calendar**: Plan your content over a quarter or a year, with topics aligned to your thought leadership goals and industry trends. A calendar helps maintain consistency in publishing and keeps your audience engaged.
- **Engage with Your Audience Regularly**: Respond to comments, answer questions, and participate in discussions. Thought leadership is as much about listening as it is about sharing insights.
- **Continuously Evolve**: Regularly assess what content performs best, what your audience is interested in, and how industry trends change. Thought leadership is dynamic, and adapting your strategy over time will keep your content fresh and relevant.

Thought leadership through content creation offers executives a way to enhance their brand, share valuable insights, and establish themselves as influential voices in their industries. You can build a well-rounded thought leadership strategy that reflects your unique expertise by creating high-quality content across different formats and platforms and leveraging AI to streamline content ideation and analytics. The next chapter will discuss reputation management and how to sustain your executive brand in both positive and challenging times.

TOOLS FOR THOUGHT LEADERSHIP AND CONTENT CREATION

To effectively create and distribute high-quality content, leveraging the right tools can make a significant difference. From producing video and audio content to scheduling posts and repurposing long-form content into shorter formats, having a toolkit of reliable equipment and software will streamline your workflow and enhance the professionalism of your thought leadership content. Here's a list of recommended tools for executives looking to establish themselves as thought leaders.

1. EQUIPMENT FOR HIGH-QUALITY VIDEO AND AUDIO CONTENT

Since visual and audio quality is essential for engaging, professional content, investing in the right equipment can elevate your presence across various platforms.

CAMERA OPTIONS

- **4K Camera for High-Resolution Video**: A 4K camera captures high-resolution video, ideal for professional-quality content.
- **Recommended Options**:
- **Sony ZV-1**: Known for its compact design, 4K resolution, and advanced autofocus, it is ideal for talking-head videos.
- **Canon EOS M50 Mark II**: A versatile mirrorless camera with excellent video quality, particularly well-suited for vlogging and webinars.
- One of my new favorites is the DJI Osmo Pocket 3 Creator Combo, a Vlogging Camera with 1″ CMOS, 4K/120fps Video, 3-Axis Stabilization, Face/Object Tracking, Fast Focusing, Mic Included for Clear Sound, Digital Camera for Photography.

- **Smartphone with 4K Video**: Many high-end smartphones now offer impressive video quality and are convenient for on-the-go content.
- **Recommended Options**:
- **iPhone 13 Pro or later**: Offers 4K resolution, strong image stabilization, and user-friendly editing tools.
- **Samsung Galaxy S21 Ultra or later**: Equipped with a 108MP sensor and 4K video recording, making it highly competitive with standalone cameras.
- If you go with this option, I recommend a 2 Pack Wireless Microphone with a battery case for iPhone, iPad, and Android. Clear and stable audio. Lightning/USB-C. There are many brands out there.

MICROPHONES FOR PROFESSIONAL SOUND QUALITY

- **Lavalier Microphone**: A lapel microphone captures clear audio while remaining discreet for on-camera work or public speaking.
- **Recommended Options: Rode Lavalier GO** or **Sennheiser MKE 2** for reliable, high-quality sound.
- **USB or Condenser Microphone**: For podcasts, webinars, and video recording, a high-quality condenser microphone captures rich audio with minimal background noise.
- **Recommended Options**:
- **Blue Yeti USB Microphone**: Known for its versatility and sound quality, suitable for podcasting and voice-overs.
- **Audio-Technica AT2020**: Offers professional-grade sound quality and works well for both voice and music recording.

LIGHTING EQUIPMENT

- **Ring Light**: Provides even, flattering lighting for videos and photos, essential for creating professional-looking content.
- **Recommended Option: Neewer 18" Ring Light** offers adjustable brightness and color temperature.
- **Softbox Lights**: For larger setups or interviews, softbox lighting kits provide soft, diffused light.
- **Recommended Option**: The **Fovitec Softbox Kit** provides two softbox lights for a balanced lighting setup.

2. SOFTWARE TOOLS FOR CONTENT CREATION AND EDITING

Creating high-quality content involves not only capturing it but also enhancing it through editing. Here are software tools for video, audio, and graphic editing.

VIDEO EDITING SOFTWARE

- **Adobe Premiere Pro**: Industry-standard software with robust editing features for long-form and short-form videos.
- **Features**: Multi-track editing, color correction, and compatibility with After Effects for advanced animations.
- **Final Cut Pro**: Apple's professional video editing software, known for its user-friendly interface and powerful features.
- **Best For**: Executives primarily using Mac products; ideal for editing high-quality video content.
- **DaVinci Resolve**: A free, high-quality video editing tool with advanced color grading and audio post-production capabilities.
- **Best For**: Professional-looking videos on a budget.

AUDIO EDITING SOFTWARE

- **Audacity**: A free, open-source tool that's ideal for recording and editing podcasts, webinars, or voice-overs.
- **Best For**: Basic audio editing, noise reduction, and sound mixing.
- **Adobe Audition**: A powerful audio editing tool with advanced sound mixing and cleanup features.
- **Best For**: Professional sound editing and noise reduction, ideal for podcasting and webinar production.

GRAPHIC DESIGN AND CONTENT CREATION TOOLS

- **Canva Pro**: A user-friendly design tool for creating social media graphics, presentations, infographics, and other visual assets.
- **Features**: Ready-made templates for social posts, presentations, and thumbnails; customization with drag-and-drop editing.
- **Adobe Spark**: Part of the Adobe suite, this tool offers a streamlined interface for creating visuals, social media posts, and short videos.
- **Best For**: Executives looking to create polished graphics and simple videos without advanced design skills.

3. CONTENT REPURPOSING TOOLS FOR MAXIMIZING REACH

Repurposing long-form content (such as interviews or webinars) into short snippets or highlights can extend its lifespan and reach new audiences.

CONTENT REPURPOSING TOOLS

- **Descript**: A versatile tool that transcribes, edits, and repurposes video and audio content, making it easy to create short clips from longer videos.
- **Best For**: Executives looking to create "highlight reels" or social media clips from podcasts, webinars, or interviews.

- **Kapwing**: A free online video editor that lets you create short, engaging clips, add subtitles, and format videos for social media.
- **Best For**: Quickly editing videos and repurposing content for platforms like Instagram, LinkedIn, and TikTok.
- **Headliner**: Specifically designed for creating shareable audio clips and audiograms, ideal for podcast snippets.
- **Best For**: Converting podcast episodes into visually engaging snippets for social media.

4. SCHEDULING AND DISTRIBUTION TOOLS

Effective thought leadership requires a consistent presence, which is best achieved with scheduling tools. These tools allow you to plan and distribute content efficiently across multiple platforms.

SOCIAL MEDIA SCHEDULING TOOLS

- **Hootsuite**: A robust platform that lets you schedule posts, track engagement, and manage multiple accounts from one dashboard.
- **Best For**: Executives managing multiple social channels; includes analytics to track performance.
- **Buffer**: A simpler, user-friendly scheduling tool offering analytics to track content performance.
- **Best For**: Scheduling and optimizing posts across LinkedIn, Twitter, Facebook, and Instagram.
- **Sprout Social**: Known for its advanced analytics, scheduling, and collaboration tools, Sprout Social is popular with larger organizations.
- **Best For**: Data-driven content strategies and in-depth social media performance analysis.

EMAIL NEWSLETTER PLATFORMS

- **LinkedIn Newsletter**: LinkedIn's built-in newsletter feature allows you to create and distribute regular content to your network directly on the platform.
- **Best For**: Building a direct, loyal following among LinkedIn connections.
- **Mailchimp**: A popular email marketing platform that's easy to use and ideal for creating branded newsletters.
- **Best For**: Executives who want to reach their audience via email with high-quality visuals and analytics.
- **Substack**: A platform for publishing newsletters and blogs, offering monetization options for premium content.
- **Best For**: Executives looking to build a subscriber base or offer exclusive content to their audience.

5. AI TOOLS FOR CONTENT IDEATION, CREATION, AND OPTIMIZATION

AI tools are invaluable for executives looking to streamline content ideation, generate ideas, and even draft content quickly. Here are some powerful AI tools for content creation and strategy.

AI CONTENT IDEATION TOOLS

- **Jasper.ai**: A popular AI writing tool that can generate ideas, write social media posts, and even help with articles.
- **Best For**: Generating blog post ideas, LinkedIn posts, or even scripts for webinars.
- **ChatGPT by OpenAI**: This versatile AI tool can suggest topics, help draft content, and provide summaries.
- **Best For**: Quick drafts, brainstorming sessions, and refining existing content ideas.

AI-DRIVEN CONTENT CREATION AND EDITING TOOLS

- **Grammarly**: An AI-powered writing assistant that corrects grammar, refines tone, and improves readability.
- **Best For**: Ensuring professional writing quality for articles, social posts, and email communications.
- **Canva Magic Write**: Canva's AI writing tool within its content creation suite; great for generating text-based content ideas.
- **Best For**: Supplementing visual content with quick, AI-suggested copy for presentations or social media posts.

ANALYTICS AND INSIGHTS

- **Google Analytics**: Track the performance of your content on your website or blog, including user behavior, engagement, and top-performing topics.
- **Best For**: Understanding audience interests and adapting content strategy accordingly.
- **LinkedIn Analytics**: Use LinkedIn's built-in analytics to monitor post-performance, audience demographics, and engagement trends.
- **Best For**: Optimizing content based on engagement levels and tracking the growth of thought leadership influence.

PUTTING IT ALL TOGETHER: BUILDING YOUR THOUGHT LEADERSHIP TOOLKIT

With the right tools, you can streamline the content creation process, maintain a consistent posting schedule, and engage your audience effectively. Here is a simple workflow to get started:

- **Ideate and Plan**: Use AI tools like Jasper or ChatGPT to generate content ideas and build a content calendar.

- **Create High-Quality Content**: Capture videos or record audio using a 4K camera or smartphone, high-quality microphone, and adequate lighting. Edit with tools like Adobe Premiere Pro or Audacity.
- **Repurpose and Schedule**: Repurpose long-form content into shorter snippets using tools like Descript or Headliner. Schedule posts in advance with Hootsuite or Buffer.
- **Monitor and Optimize**: Use LinkedIn Analytics, Google Analytics, or platform-specific metrics to track engagement and refine your strategy over time.

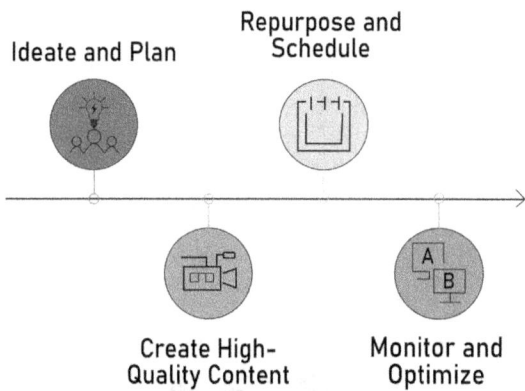

Content creation and Management Process

By investing in the right equipment and software, executives can streamline content creation, produce high-quality work, and effectively reach their target audience. Leveraging AI tools further enhances this process by providing inspiration, automating certain tasks, and analyzing engagement, enabling you to focus on delivering meaningful, value-driven content.

UNLOCK THE MAGIC—
SCAN, TO LEARN MORE!

8

LEVERAGING PUBLIC SPEAKING AND MEDIA APPEARANCES

THE POWER OF PUBLIC SPEAKING AND MEDIA ENGAGEMENTS FOR EXECUTIVE BRANDING

Public speaking and media appearances are powerful tools for executives looking to strengthen their personal brand, expand their influence, and engage with wider audiences. Speaking at conferences, industry panels, and company events positions you as a thought leader, offering a platform to demonstrate authority and showcase your expertise. Likewise, media engagements—such as interviews, podcast guest spots, and appearances on business news segments—amplify your message and extend your reach, further solidifying your executive brand in the public eye.

This chapter will explore the benefits of public speaking and media engagements for executive branding, providing actionable strategies to help you become a sought-after speaker, handle media interviews effectively, and deliver impactful, memorable messages.

WHY PUBLIC SPEAKING AND MEDIA ENGAGEMENTS MATTER FOR EXECUTIVES

For executives, visibility in public forums and media channels plays a critical role in shaping brand reputation, credibility, and professional influence. Here's why these engagements are essential for executive branding:

- **Reinforcing Brand Authority**: Regular public appearances and media engagements position you as an authority in your field, enhancing your personal brand.
- **Amplifying Reach**: Media coverage and public speaking broaden your influence, helping you connect with audiences beyond your immediate network.

- **Enhancing Credibility**: Appearances in reputable media outlets or speaking at respected industry events lend credibility to your expertise, making your brand more trustworthy.
- **Building Connections with Key Stakeholders**: Public speaking and media engagements offer opportunities to connect with other industry leaders, stakeholders, and potential clients or collaborators.

1. BECOMING A SOUGHT-AFTER SPEAKER

To become a sought-after speaker, it's essential to build a strong reputation that aligns with your expertise and thought leadership goals. This process involves positioning yourself as a valuable resource within your industry while cultivating a unique perspective that resonates with your audience. Here's a closer look at the steps to help you establish yourself as a sought-after speaker:

IDENTIFY YOUR NICHE AND EXPERTISE

A clearly defined niche and specialized expertise are key to standing out in a competitive landscape. When event organizers select speakers, they seek professionals who offer unique insights and in-depth knowledge. By identifying your niche and emphasizing your unique value proposition (UVP), you can craft a consistent message that makes you both memorable and relevant.

CLARIFY YOUR UNIQUE VALUE PROPOSITION (UVP)

- **Define Your Core Expertise**: Consider the areas where you have deep knowledge, proven experience, and insights that set you apart. Ask yourself what specific value you bring that others might not. This could be industry experience, technical expertise, or a unique perspective on trends and challenges within your field.
- **Identify Key Audience Needs**: Consider the challenges, pain points, or emerging opportunities within your industry that your

expertise can address. Your UVP should showcase your strengths and connect to the real-world issues that audiences care about.
- **Emphasize Unique Insights**: Focus on what makes your approach or experience unique. For instance, an executive with experience in AI implementation may emphasize practical insights on "AI for Business Growth" or explore ethical considerations in "Responsible AI in Leadership."

Example: A finance executive specializing in risk management might define their UVP around "Building Resilient Organizations," drawing on experience managing financial crises and positioning themselves as a resource for businesses seeking stability in volatile times.

CHOOSE A CLEAR, CONSISTENT MESSAGE

- **Identify Core Themes**: Decide on the main themes that align with your expertise and your target audience's interests. These themes should be broad enough for multiple presentations or talks but specific enough to define your brand identity. Consider what you want to be known for—digital innovation, sustainability, or inclusive leadership.
- **Align with Industry Trends**: Choose themes that resonate with current trends and emerging topics within your industry. For instance, if cybersecurity is a growing concern, a technology executive might focus on "Future-Proofing Business Against Cyber Threats" as a core message.
- **Reflect Your Brand and Values**: Your message should authentically represent your personal and professional brand. You reinforce your brand identity by consistently aligning with your values, making your talks more impactful and memorable.

Example: A healthcare executive could choose "Transforming Patient Care through Technology" as a core message, tapping into current trends in digital health and aligning with their mission to improve patient outcomes.

FOCUS ON HIGH-IMPACT TOPICS

- **Address Pressing Industry Issues**: High-impact topics are those that tackle key challenges, trends, or innovations within your field. Research the common pain points and needs of your audience, as well as emerging trends and shifts in the industry. By concentrating on these topics, you position yourself as a thought leader who offers valuable and relevant insights.
- **Prioritize Actionable Takeaways**: High-impact topics should not only highlight important issues but also provide solutions or actionable steps. Audiences and organizers value speakers who offer practical, implementable advice rather than abstract theories.
- **Evolve with Market Demands**: Stay updated on changes within your industry to ensure your topics remain relevant. Being agile and adapting your message to reflect new developments—such as regulatory changes or technological advancements—helps you remain at the forefront of industry discussions.

Example: A technology executive with expertise in digital transformation could focus on a topic like "Future-Proofing Business through Technology." This topic appeals to leaders across industries by addressing the universal need for adaptability in a rapidly evolving digital landscape.

BUILD YOUR SPEAKING PORTFOLIO

Creating a visible portfolio of speaking engagements is essential for establishing your credibility as a speaker. Your portfolio not only highlights your experience but also showcases your speaking style and areas of expertise, making it easier for event organizers to assess your fit for their event.

- **Start with Smaller Engagements**: Begin by participating in local events, industry meetups, webinars, or guest lectures. These smaller engagements provide an opportunity to build experience and refine your speaking skills. They also allow you to experiment with different presentation styles and fine-tune your message without the pressure of a large audience.
- **Create a Speaker Reel**: Compile high-quality video clips of your past presentations to showcase your speaking style, energy, and impact. A well-crafted speaker reel gives event organizers a clear sense of your delivery and reinforces your expertise.
- **Build a Professional Speaker Page**: Dedicate a section on your website or LinkedIn profile to highlight your speaking engagements, topics, and achievements. Include your speaker reel, biography, and testimonials to provide a comprehensive overview of your qualifications.

Example: An executive might start by speaking at regional conferences or company events. Over time, they can use these experiences to create a speaker reel and professional page. As their reputation grows, they can pitch themselves for larger conferences and industry-wide events.

PROACTIVELY NETWORK AND PITCH FOR SPEAKING OPPORTUNITIES

Building a reputation as a sought-after speaker often involves actively pursuing and securing speaking opportunities. Networking and strategic pitching can help you connect with event organizers and position yourself as a valuable speaker for upcoming events.

- **Network with Event Organizers and Industry Leaders**: Attend conferences, participate in webinars, and connect with industry

leaders and event organizers. Building relationships within the industry helps you stay informed about speaking opportunities and increases the likelihood of receiving recommendations.
- **Leverage LinkedIn and Other Professional Networks**: Sharing insights, articles, and thought leadership content on LinkedIn or industry forums can help establish your authority and attract the attention of event organizers. Engage with posts, join relevant groups, and participate in conversations to boost your visibility.
- **Develop a Compelling Speaker Pitch**: Prepare a concise and compelling pitch that outlines your expertise, speaking topics, and the unique value you offer to audiences. Tailor your pitch for each event to highlight how your message aligns with the event's theme and the needs of its audience.

Example: A marketing executive with expertise in digital branding might join LinkedIn groups for marketing professionals, regularly share insights, and engage with posts from conference organizers. When pitching themselves as a speaker, they could focus on topics like "Building a Personal Brand in the Digital Age," emphasizing their experience and relevance to the audience.

BECOMING RECOGNIZABLE AS A GO-TO EXPERT

As you establish yourself as a speaker, your goal is to become recognized as the go-to expert in your niche. Consistent messaging, high-impact topics, and a visible portfolio all contribute to building a recognizable brand that naturally attracts speaking opportunities. Over time, as your reputation grows, event organizers may reach out directly, solidifying your status as a sought-after speaker in your field.

2. PREPARING FOR CONFERENCES AND DELIVERING IMPACTFUL MESSAGES

Once you've secured a speaking engagement, thorough preparation is key to ensuring that your presentation is compelling, memorable, and reinforces your executive brand. The goal is to deliver a message that resonates with your audience and positions you as a thought leader in your field. This requires understanding your audience, structuring your presentation strategically, and practicing to build both confidence and adaptability.

RESEARCH THE AUDIENCE AND EVENT GOALS

Understanding both your audience and the event's objectives is fundamental to delivering a meaningful presentation. Tailoring your content to align with the audience's needs and the event's themes not only enhances the impact of your message but also ensures it is well-received.

UNDERSTAND AUDIENCE EXPECTATIONS

- **Analyze Audience Demographics**: Research who will be attending, including their professional backgrounds, industries, and roles. Are they senior executives, mid-level managers, or emerging leaders? Knowing the demographics allows you to adjust the complexity and focus of your message accordingly.
- **Identify Key Interests and Pain Points**: Consider the challenges or trends most relevant to your audience. Reviewing the event's promotional materials, agenda, or speaker lineup can provide insight into what topics are likely to resonate with them.
- **Adapt Your Tone and Style**: For a formal audience, a data-driven and structured approach might be most effective. For a younger or more creative crowd, a conversational and interactive style could engage them more successfully.

Example: If you're speaking at an HR conference primarily attended by mid-level HR managers, focus on practical leadership strategies for managing diverse teams. This would be more relevant and actionable than discussing high-level executive strategies, ensuring your talk speaks directly to this group's needs.

ALIGN WITH EVENT THEMES

- **Study the Event's Theme**: Conferences often revolve around a central theme, such as "Innovation in Leadership" or "Sustainable Business Practices." Tailoring your message to this theme helps your presentation integrate smoothly with the overall event, increasing its relevance and impact.
- **Reflect Your Brand and Values within the Theme**: Ensure that your message remains consistent with your personal brand and core values. For example, if the theme is "Technology and the Future" and your area of expertise is ethical AI, you could position your message around "The Ethical Future of AI." This approach ensures that you stay true to your brand while aligning with the event's focus.

Example: At a sustainability-focused conference, an executive with expertise in supply chain management might adapt their message by discussing topics like "Green Supply Chains" or "Sustainable Procurement Practices." This shows how their expertise aligns with the event's mission, while contributing valuable insights on the theme.

COORDINATE WITH OTHER SPEAKERS

- **Connect with Panelists or Fellow Speakers**: If you're part of a panel or session with other speakers, connect with them beforehand. Discuss your key points and agree on any overlapping areas to ensure each person's contribution is unique and complementary.

- **Understand the Flow of the Session**: For panel discussions or co-hosted presentations, knowing the flow of the session helps you pace your points and ensures smooth transitions. Working collaboratively fosters a more engaging, cohesive experience for the audience.
- **Anticipate Shared Questions**: Coordinating with other speakers can also help you anticipate questions directed to the entire panel, allowing you to prepare thoughtful responses.

Example: For a leadership panel, an executive focused on team innovation might coordinate with other speakers who cover change management or conflict resolution, creating a more holistic view of leadership for the audience.

CRAFT A COMPELLING PRESENTATION

A well-structured, engaging presentation captures and holds the audience's attention while effectively delivering your key message. Thoughtful organization, relatable storytelling, and impactful visuals are critical to achieving this.

STRUCTURE WITH A CLEAR MESSAGE FLOW

- **Start with an Engaging Introduction**: Open with a story, surprising statistic, or question that captures attention and sets the stage for your topic. This initial hook should be directly relevant to your audience and the key message of your presentation.
- **Organize with Logical Segments**: Break down your presentation into logical segments with clear transitions between them. This approach helps the audience follow your train of thought and keeps the message clear and organized.
- **Conclude with Actionable Takeaways**: End by summarizing key points and providing actionable steps or insights. A strong

closing reinforces your message and gives the audience something concrete to remember.

Example: In a presentation on digital transformation, an executive might start with a relatable story about a challenge they faced in adopting new technology, structure the talk around three main points (challenges, solutions, outcomes), and conclude with specific advice for implementing digital change.

INCORPORATE STORIES AND CASE STUDIES

- **Use Personal Stories for Connection**: Audiences tend to remember stories far more than raw facts. Share relevant personal experiences or challenges you've overcome. This approach humanizes your presentation and helps make your message more relatable.
- **Highlight Industry-Specific Case Studies**: If personal stories aren't available, consider using case studies that illustrate your points. Case studies provide concrete examples of your message in action, adding both credibility and depth to your presentation.
- **Tie Stories to Core Message Points**: Every story or case study should serve to reinforce your key messages. This approach helps anchor abstract ideas in real-world situations, making them easier for your audience to grasp.

Example: A finance executive discussing financial strategy might reference a case study of a company that successfully navigated a financial downturn. By showing how strategic adjustments led to measurable outcomes, the executive can connect each step to actionable takeaways.

ENGAGE WITH VISUALS AND MINIMAL TEXT

- **Prioritize High-Quality, Relevant Visuals**: Use images, infographics, and charts that not only enhance understanding but also emphasize key points. Avoid cluttered or overly complex visuals, as they can distract from your message and confuse the audience.
- **Limit Text on Slides**: Keep your slides simple and text-light. Think of them as a guide rather than a script. Use bullet points or short phrases that reinforce what you're saying, but avoid overwhelming the viewer with too much text.
- **Use Visual Cues to Reinforce Key Points**: Utilize elements like color-coding, icons, or bolding important terms to help direct the audience's attention to specific points. Visual cues assist in guiding the audience and improving retention of key insights.

Example: A healthcare executive discussing patient care might incorporate an infographic showing patient satisfaction statistics or outcomes. This allows the audience to easily visualize the impact of various care strategies without needing lengthy explanations.

PRACTICE FOR CONFIDENCE AND FLEXIBILITY

Effective practice helps you deliver your presentation confidently and seamlessly, preparing you to handle unexpected changes or audience questions. It also ensures you stay within your allotted time, showing respect for both the audience and event organizers.

REHEARSE WITH A TIMER

- **Practice Multiple Times**: Run through your presentation several times, ideally in front of colleagues or friends who can offer constructive feedback. Practicing with a timer ensures you stay within the time limit, leaving room for Q&A if applicable.

- **Time Each Section**: Break down your presentation into sections and time each one to avoid spending too long on any single point. This pacing maintains balance and ensures all key points are covered.
- **Simulate Real Conditions**: Practice in conditions similar to the actual event. For example, stand while presenting, or practice in front of a mirror to observe your body language and expressions.

Example: If you have 20 minutes for your talk, aim to finish around the 18-minute mark to allow time for a question or two. Time your introduction, main points, and conclusion to stay on track and avoid feeling rushed.

PREPARE FOR POTENTIAL QUESTIONS

- **Anticipate Common or Challenging Questions**: Consider the questions likely to arise, especially those that may require specific or sensitive answers. Preparing answers to these questions helps you respond with confidence.
- **Practice Concise Responses**: Ensure that your answers are concise and to the point. Rambling responses can undermine your authority, so focus on delivering clear, confident answers.
- **Be Ready for Tough Questions**: Occasionally, audience members may ask challenging or provocative questions. Practice staying composed, acknowledging the question, and responding diplomatically.

Example: An executive discussing crisis management might prepare answers to common questions about handling PR issues or maintaining morale during tough times, allowing them to address these effectively and demonstrate expertise.

STAY ADAPTABLE

- **Be Prepared for Last-Minute Adjustments**: Sometimes, events run behind schedule or sessions are shortened. Plan to adapt your presentation by knowing which points can be skipped or condensed if necessary.
- **Embrace Q&A Opportunities**: If the event turns into more of a Q&A session, adjust accordingly. This can offer a unique opportunity for deeper interaction with the audience, showcasing your flexibility and knowledge on the spot.
- **Keep a Positive Attitude**: Adaptability is as much about mindset as it is about preparation. Embrace any unexpected changes as opportunities to demonstrate your expertise and flexibility, rather than seeing them as disruptions.

Example: If your presentation on crisis management is shortened, focus on your key takeaways and be prepared to answer questions about specific challenges, rather than rushing through all planned content. This allows you to still provide value without feeling rushed.

FINAL THOUGHTS ON PREPARING FOR CONFERENCES

Preparation is the cornerstone of delivering an impactful presentation that resonates with your audience and strengthens your brand. By thoroughly researching your audience, crafting a clear and engaging presentation, and practicing effectively, you'll be ready to deliver a memorable message that establishes you as a thought leader. Well-executed preparation also boosts your confidence and adaptability, enabling you to navigate unexpected changes and engage meaningfully with your audience.

3. HANDLING MEDIA INTERVIEWS AND ENGAGING WITH THE PRESS

Media interviews—whether with industry publications, business news channels, or podcasts—are powerful platforms for executive branding. A well-handled interview can significantly elevate your credibility, broaden your reach, and reinforce your thought leadership. Successful media engagement hinges on thorough preparation, clear communication, and cultivating relationships with journalists and media outlets over time.

PREPARE KEY TALKING POINTS

Before any media interview, defining the key messages you want to convey is essential. Having clear talking points ensures your responses align with your executive brand and provides a foundation for handling unexpected or challenging questions.

DEFINE YOUR CORE MESSAGE

- **Identify Main Themes**: Determine the central message you want to convey, emphasizing areas that highlight your expertise and reinforce your brand. Whether it's sustainability, innovation, or corporate culture, your message should be clear and relevant to both your goals and the topic at hand.
- **Align with Brand Values**: Every response should reflect your values and brand identity. For example, if inclusivity is central to your brand, find ways to weave this theme into your answers—even if the interview doesn't directly focus on it.
- **Highlight Unique Insights**: Think about what unique perspective you bring to the topic. This could be an unconventional approach, a personal anecdote, or specific experiences that add depth and distinguish your message from others in the field.

Example: If an executive specializing in digital transformation is interviewed about emerging technology trends, they might focus on their belief in ethical AI, underscoring how their company's approach balances technological innovation with societal impact.

ANTICIPATE QUESTIONS

- **Consider Likely and Challenging Questions**: Prepare for both common questions about your field and potentially challenging ones, especially if the topic is sensitive or controversial. Having prepared responses to tough questions allows you to address them confidently and maintain control over the conversation.
- **Prepare for Unexpected Follow-Up Questions**: Journalists may ask follow-up questions based on your responses. Anticipate how these could evolve and be ready to elaborate on your points while staying aligned with your core message.
- **Stay Informed on Relevant Topics**: If the interview will touch on current trends or industry challenges, ensure you're up-to-date on the latest developments. This will allow you to provide timely, informed answers.

Example: If interviewed about corporate social responsibility, an executive might prepare answers to potential questions on specific company practices, industry trends, or criticisms of certain CSR approaches, ensuring they can address both the positive and challenging aspects effectively.

FOCUS ON VALUE FOR THE AUDIENCE

- **Emphasize Actionable Insights**: Audiences and journalists value interviews that provide practical takeaways or thought-provoking ideas. Frame your answers to offer valuable insights that listeners can apply or reflect on.
- **Avoid Over-Promotion**: The interview should not solely serve as an opportunity to promote your company or achievements.

Instead, focus on how your insights can benefit the audience or address industry-wide issues.
- **Be Genuine and Transparent**: Authenticity resonates with audiences. Don't hesitate to acknowledge challenges or learning experiences, as these can enhance your credibility and relatability.

Example: If an executive is interviewed on sustainability practices, they might discuss their company's innovative recycling program while providing broader advice for companies aiming to reduce their environmental impact. This approach keeps the focus on providing value while subtly highlighting the executive's expertise.

PRACTICE EFFECTIVE COMMUNICATION TECHNIQUES

Clear and effective communication is critical in media interviews, as journalists often seek concise, memorable responses. Practicing communication techniques ensures your points are impactful and resonate with both the interviewer and the audience.

BE CLEAR AND CONCISE

- **Aim for Brevity**: Journalists often prefer shorter, direct answers. Aim to convey your points in clear, concise sentences, avoiding jargon or overly complex language.
- **Answer with Purpose: Each answer should support your core message. Avoid tangents and keep responses aligned with your brand and the topic.**
- **Practice for Fluidity**: Practice delivering responses smoothly and confidently. This helps you avoid filler words like "um" or "you know," which can detract from your authority.

Example: If an executive is asked how their company approaches innovation, they might respond with, "Innovation for us is about empowering our teams to experiment. We create an environment where failure is a learning opportunity, driving continuous improvement."

USE SOUND BITES

- **Craft Memorable Statements**: Prepare a few sound bites—short, impactful statements that summarize your key points in a way that's easy to remember and quote. These statements are often picked up in headlines or used as key quotes in articles.
- **Balance Insight and Simplicity**: A sound bite should be both insightful and accessible. Avoid overly technical language or jargon, and focus on expressing your idea in a way that resonates with a broad audience.
- **Deliver with Confidence**: Sound bites are most effective when delivered with clear emphasis and pacing. Practice delivering them confidently to make them stand out.

Example: In a live interview about company growth, an executive might prepare a sound bite like, "At our company, growth isn't just about profits; it's about creating a future where both our people and communities can thrive."

STAY CALM AND COMPOSED

- **Pause Before Responding**: Taking a moment before answering allows you to gather your thoughts and respond thoughtfully, especially to challenging or unexpected questions. Pausing can also add emphasis to your response.
- **Pivot Back to Core Message**: If the question strays from your intended message, subtly pivot back to your core points. Acknowledge the question, then redirect the focus to your main message or key insights.
- **Remain Professional under Pressure**: Some questions may be challenging or even confrontational. Maintain a calm demeanor,

keep your tone respectful, and focus on providing balanced, informative responses.

Example: If asked about a controversial company decision, an executive might acknowledge the question, then pivot with, "While there are always challenges, we focus on solutions that benefit our stakeholders in the long term. Our decisions are guided by a commitment to sustainability and growth."

BUILD RELATIONSHIPS WITH JOURNALISTS AND MEDIA OUTLETS

Cultivating positive relationships with journalists and editors can enhance your media presence and establish you as a reliable source for expert commentary. These connections also increase the likelihood of being called upon for future stories or industry insights.

CONNECT WITH INDUSTRY REPORTERS

- **Engage on Social Media**: Engage on social media by following journalists who cover topics related to your expertise. Engage with their posts by liking, sharing, or commenting thoughtfully, building familiarity over time.
- **Offer Insights on Relevant Topics**: When appropriate, reach out to journalists with a quick message or comment on their work, offering insights or expressing appreciation for their coverage. This opens the door for future connections.
- **Showcase Your Expertise on LinkedIn**: Share articles, posts, and insights on LinkedIn to demonstrate your knowledge. Journalists often use LinkedIn to find subject matter experts, which may lead to interview opportunities.

Example: An executive in healthcare might follow journalists who cover health policy or innovation, occasionally sharing their articles with a comment that provides additional insight. This interaction helps the journalist recognize the executive as an informed source in their field.

OFFER FOLLOW-UP INFORMATION

- **Provide Additional Resources**: After the interview, offer the journalist any supplementary resources or insights that could add depth to their story, such as data, reports, or links to relevant content.
- **Thank the Journalist**: Send a brief thank-you message expressing appreciation for the opportunity and acknowledging their professionalism. This small gesture builds rapport and increases the likelihood of future collaborations.
- **Offer Availability for Future Stories**: Let the journalist know you're open to providing insight for future stories on related topics, reinforcing your position as a valuable, knowledgeable source.

Example: After an interview on sustainability, an executive might send the journalist a link to a company report or industry study that adds context to the discussion. A brief thank-you note further solidifies the relationship.

BE AVAILABLE FOR TIMELY TOPICS

- **Stay Informed and Ready to Comment**: Media often seeks expert commentary on breaking news. You can quickly offer relevant insights by staying informed on current events and industry developments, positioning yourself as a go-to expert.
- **Respond Promptly to Media Inquiries**: Timely responses to media requests demonstrate reliability and make it more likely that journalists will reach out again in the future.
- **Provide Thoughtful, Balanced Commentary**: Avoid taking extreme positions unless relevant to your brand when commenting

on breaking news. Focus on balanced, insightful commentary that adds depth to the story.

Example: If you're a healthcare executive and a new health policy is announced, being available to provide timely commentary on its potential industry impact can establish you as a reliable media contact. A well-thought-out, balanced response ensures your comments are viewed as credible and informative.

Media interviews are key to building your executive brand and expanding industry influence. By preparing, practicing communication techniques, and cultivating relationships with journalists, you ensure your responses reinforce your brand, resonate with the audience, and position you as a credible thought leader, opening doors for future media opportunities.

4. LEVERAGING RECORDED TALKS AND MEDIA APPEARANCES FOR BRAND REINFORCEMENT

Media interviews, speaking engagements, and other appearances have lasting value beyond the initial event. By repurposing recorded talks, media appearances, and interview highlights, you can extend the reach of your message, amplify your brand, and continually engage with new audiences. This ongoing content is a portfolio of your expertise, reinforcing your credibility and thought leadership.

SHARE RECORDINGS AND HIGHLIGHTS ON SOCIAL MEDIA

Sharing full recordings and highlights on social media platforms like LinkedIn, YouTube, Twitter, and Instagram extends the impact of your media appearances. It keeps your network informed about your latest insights. This practice maximizes your reach and keeps your brand active and visible across multiple channels.

POST ON LINKEDIN AND TWITTER

- **Share Full Recordings or Key Takeaways**: When sharing a full recording or highlight reel, include context about why the topic is important or how it connects to your expertise. This helps your audience understand the relevance and adds value to the content.
- **Pin or Feature on Profiles**: On LinkedIn, YouTube, and Twitter, you can pin the post to the top of your profile, giving it prolonged visibility. This is especially useful for significant talks or interviews you want to highlight for an extended period.
- **Tag Relevant People or Organizations**: Tag them in your post if you collaborated with others or spoke at a particular event. This can increase engagement as they may reshare or comment, expanding the reach of their networks as well.

Example: After delivering a keynote at a digital transformation conference, an executive could post the full recording on LinkedIn with a caption like, "Grateful to have shared insights on adapting to digital change at [Event Name]. Here's why embracing innovation is essential for growth in 2024."

CREATE SHORT VIDEO CLIPS FOR ENGAGEMENT

- **Extract Key Moments**: Identify the most engaging moments, sound bites, or insights from your appearance. Short clips of 30–60 seconds are ideal for platforms like Instagram, YouTube Shorts, and LinkedIn, where attention spans are shorter.
- **Add Captions or Graphics**: Include captions to make your content more accessible and visually appealing. Simple graphics or branded templates can help maintain consistency and make clips easily recognizable.
- **Encourage Audience Interaction**: Add a call to action to encourage viewers to comment, ask questions, or share their thoughts. This

interaction can boost engagement and bring new followers to your profile.

Example: An executive discussing leadership in a panel might create a short clip of their answer to a key question, such as "What's the biggest leadership challenge today?" Captioned with "How leaders can overcome today's biggest challenge," this clip could encourage discussions in the comments.

ADD CONTENT TO YOUR WEBSITE

- **Embed Videos and Audio Clips**: Create a dedicated "Media" or "Insights" section on your website where visitors can access your recorded talks, podcast interviews, and media features. This builds a comprehensive expertise archive and adds depth to your professional portfolio.
- **Include Written Summaries or Transcripts**: For added SEO benefits and accessibility, include a written summary or transcript of each video or audio clip. This makes your content searchable and easily accessible for those who prefer reading over watching or listening.
- **Highlight Featured Content**: If a particularly notable appearance—such as a high-profile panel or a keynote speech—features it prominently on your homepage or professional bio section.

Example: An executive who frequently speaks on economic policy might have a "Media & Insights" page that includes recordings, summaries, and transcripts of talks, organized by topic for easy navigation.

REPURPOSE CONTENT FOR ARTICLES AND NEWSLETTERS

Repurposing media appearances into written content, such as articles and newsletter summaries, can reach an even broader audience. Written content is easily shareable and can provide more depth for those who prefer reading or want a concise version of the full talk.

WRITE AN ARTICLE BASED ON YOUR TALK

- **Summarize Key Insights**: Turn your presentation or interview into an article by distilling the main takeaways into a clear, structured piece. This is especially useful for those who missed the live event but want to engage with the core ideas.
- **Use a Catchy Title**: Titles like "5 Strategies for Navigating Economic Change" or "The Future of AI in Business" can help grab attention and clearly communicate the value of the content.
- **Share on LinkedIn and Blog Platforms**: Publish your article on LinkedIn, Medium, or your personal blog, then share it across your social media platforms. This cross-posting helps increase visibility and drives traffic to your profile or website.

Example: An executive who gave a talk on resilience during economic uncertainty could write a LinkedIn article titled "5 Resilience Strategies for Leaders Facing Economic Challenges," summarizing their key points and providing actionable advice.

INCLUDE IN NEWSLETTERS

- **Feature Summaries of Recent Talks**: If you send out regular newsletters, include a summary or highlights from recent talks and media appearances. This keeps your audience up-to-date and reinforces your brand.

- **Link to Full Recordings or Articles**: Provide links to full recordings, transcripts, or blog posts so readers can explore further if interested. This increases traffic to your media portfolio and keeps subscribers engaged with your content.
- **Offer Exclusive Insights or Takeaways**: Consider adding a few "bonus" insights or behind-the-scenes anecdotes that did not make it into the talk. This added value gives subscribers an incentive to stay engaged with your newsletter.

Example: An executive could feature their recent podcast interview on leadership challenges in their monthly newsletter, linking to the full episode and summarizing key points. Adding a personal note about what inspired the discussion could increase relatability.

CREATE A RESOURCE PAGE FOR MEDIA AND SPEAKING ENGAGEMENTS

- **Organize Content by Topic or Format**: Create a "Media" or "Insights" page on your website where you compile recorded talks, written articles, podcasts, and interviews. Organize the content by topic (e.g., leadership, digital transformation) or by format to make navigation easy for visitors.
- **Add a Brief Description for Each Item**: Provide a short description for each video, article, or podcast, explaining its focus and relevance. This helps visitors decide what content to explore first.
- **Regularly Update with New Appearances**: Keep your resource page current by adding new media appearances and talks. An updated portfolio reflects your active involvement in the industry and shows commitment to your field.

Example: An executive who frequently speaks at conferences could create a "Speaking & Media" page, with categories like "Leadership Talks," "Economic Analysis," and "Corporate Strategy." Each item would link to recordings or articles, making it easy for visitors to explore their expertise.

Leveraging recorded talks and media appearances as part of your executive brand strategy not only broadens the reach of your thought leadership but also helps you cultivate a well-rounded portfolio of expertise. By sharing full recordings, repurposing key highlights, and creating accessible written content, you can keep engaging both new and existing audiences. These strategies ensure that each engagement has maximum impact, reinforcing your brand's authority and establishing you as a trusted thought leader in your field.

CHAPTER WRAP-UP

Public speaking and media engagements are invaluable tools for strengthening your executive brand, showcasing your expertise, and reaching a wider audience. By preparing thoroughly for each appearance, delivering a clear message, and strategically repurposing content, you can amplify the effectiveness of every engagement. Embracing these opportunities boosts your visibility, credibility, and authority, positioning you as a trusted thought leader in your industry. In the next chapter, we'll explore strategies for managing your reputation and handling challenging situations to maintain a robust executive brand.

UNLOCK THE MAGIC—
SCAN, TO LEARN MORE!

9

MANAGING YOUR REPUTATION

Reputation is one of the most valuable assets an executive can cultivate. In today's digital age, where information spreads instantly, maintaining a strong and consistent brand image requires proactive reputation management. A solid reputation can open doors, attract opportunities, and build trust with stakeholders, while a poorly managed reputation can result in lost business, diminished credibility, and lasting career damage.

This chapter explores the critical role of reputation management for executives, offering strategies for monitoring feedback, handling criticism constructively, and leveraging positive testimonials to build trust and reinforce credibility. By actively managing your reputation, you can maintain a brand image that authentically reflects your values, expertise, and leadership.

WHY REPUTATION MANAGEMENT MATTERS FOR EXECUTIVES

As a leader, your reputation extends beyond your personal brand to impact your company, team, and industry influence. A strong, positive reputation:

- **Builds Trust and Credibility**: Executives are held to high standards. A well-managed reputation instills confidence in employees, clients, investors, and peers, reinforcing your trustworthiness and reliability.
- **Attracts Opportunities**: A positive reputation can open doors to board seats, partnerships, speaking engagements, and media coverage. Organizations and stakeholders are more likely to collaborate with executives known for their integrity and expertise.
- **Influences Perception of Your Organization**: Your actions and behavior reflect on your organization as a whole. A reputable executive enhances the company's image, while a poorly managed reputation can negatively affect the organization's public perception.

- **Protects Against Crisis**: Reputation management is not only about building positive perceptions; it also involves crisis preparedness. By actively managing your reputation, you'll be better equipped to handle challenges and mitigate potential damage.

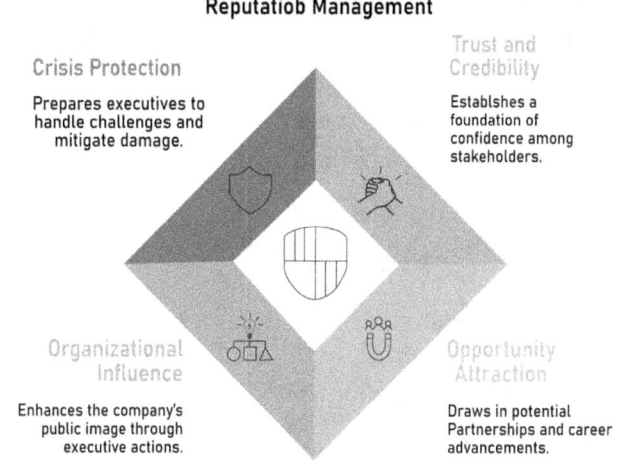

TECHNIQUES FOR MONITORING YOUR REPUTATION

Effective reputation management starts with awareness. By regularly monitoring your reputation, you can stay informed about public perceptions, identify potential risks, and take action before issues escalate.

1. SET UP GOOGLE ALERTS AND SOCIAL LISTENING TOOLS

- **Google Alerts**: Set up Google Alerts for your name, company, and any relevant keywords related to your field. This free tool notifies you whenever new content is published online, helping you track mentions in news articles, blogs, or forums.

- **Social Listening Tools**: Tools like **Brandwatch**, **Mention**, and **Hootsuite** allow you to monitor conversations about your brand on social media platforms. Social listening provides insights into how people discuss your brand and allows you to address questions or concerns in real-time.
- **Platform-Specific Monitoring**: Regularly check professional networks like LinkedIn, as well as industry-specific forums where peers, clients, or competitors may discuss your work. Staying active on these platforms helps you better understand how your brand is perceived within your field.

Example: An executive in digital marketing could set up alerts for their name, company, and terms like "digital transformation" or "marketing automation" to stay updated on discussions related to their expertise.

2. REGULARLY REVIEW PUBLIC FEEDBACK AND TESTIMONIALS

- **Analyze Reviews and Testimonials**: If you or your company have profiles on sites like Glassdoor, Google Reviews, or LinkedIn Recommendations, make it a habit to review feedback regularly. Positive testimonials reinforce your brand, while constructive criticism can provide insight into areas for improvement.
- **Seek Patterns in Feedback**: Identify recurring themes in feedback. If you notice consistent comments about your leadership style, communication, or decision-making, it could highlight areas where you're excelling—or where adjustments may be needed.
- **Acknowledge and Address Constructive Criticism**: When you receive critical reviews, respond professionally and acknowledge the feedback. Demonstrating accountability and a willingness to improve can transform a potentially negative situation into an opportunity to strengthen your reputation.

Example: A tech executive might notice recurring comments about their responsiveness in client reviews. If feedback suggests the need for faster communication, they could prioritize improving their responsiveness, showing adaptability to client needs.

3. CONDUCT PERIODIC SELF-ASSESSMENTS

- **Evaluate Your Online Presence**: Periodically review your social media profiles, personal website, and other online platforms where you're active. Ensure that all content aligns with your brand values, expertise, and image. Outdated or inconsistent information can undermine your reputation.
- **Seek Feedback from Trusted Colleagues**: Reach out to colleagues, mentors, or trusted advisors for honest feedback on your reputation. Their perspective can offer valuable insights into how others perceive you and highlight areas that might need attention.
- **Perform a SWOT Analysis**: Consider conducting a personal SWOT analysis (Strengths, Weaknesses, Opportunities, Threats) on your reputation. Recognizing areas of strength as well as potential risks can help you proactively address weaknesses.

Example: An executive could ask a mentor to review their LinkedIn profile and recent public statements, seeking feedback on how well these elements represent their professional goals and values.

RESPONDING TO CRITICISM AND NEGATIVE FEEDBACK

No matter how well-managed your brand is, criticism is inevitable. The way you handle it can either enhance or damage your reputation. Responding effectively to criticism requires a balanced approach that acknowledges concerns, offers solutions, and reinforces your commitment to improvement.

1. ACKNOWLEDGE AND OWN UP TO MISTAKES

- **Respond Promptly and Professionally**: Addressing criticism promptly shows that you take feedback seriously. Avoid becoming defensive, and respond in a way that demonstrates your openness to constructive criticism.
- **Take Responsibility When Necessary**: Take ownership of the situation if there is a legitimate concern. Acknowledging mistakes demonstrates accountability, integrity, and transparency, reinforcing trust.
- **Apologize Sincerely and Offer a Path Forward**: If an apology is warranted, express it sincerely and outline specific steps you'll take to prevent similar issues in the future.

Example: If an executive receives feedback on a delayed response time, they might acknowledge the delay, apologize, and implement a system to improve communication timeliness, reinforcing their commitment to customer satisfaction.

2. KEEP THE FOCUS ON SOLUTIONS

- **Highlight Corrective Actions**: When responding to criticism, emphasize your steps to address the issue. Demonstrating a solutions-oriented approach can reassure stakeholders that you're proactive and committed to improvement.
- **Follow Up on Resolved Issues**: After addressing the feedback, consider following up to confirm that the issue has been resolved. This demonstrates that you value feedback and have taken concrete actions to improve.
- **Avoid Escalating Conflict**: Avoid engaging in public arguments, which can further damage your reputation. Instead, keep responses respectful and focused on positive, constructive solutions.

Example: If feedback indicates that a client felt unsupported during a project, the executive could acknowledge the oversight, outline new support measures being implemented, and follow up to ensure client satisfaction moving forward.

3. REFRAME CRITICISM AS AN OPPORTUNITY

- **See Criticism as a Learning Tool**: Use criticism as a learning opportunity. Rather than viewing negative feedback as a setback, treat it as a chance to gain insights into how your actions are perceived and identify areas for improvement.
- **Share Lessons Learned**: If appropriate, publicly share how the experience led to positive changes in your approach or practices. This transparency can enhance your credibility, showing others that you embrace growth and improvement.
- **Use Criticism to Strengthen Resilience**: Handling criticism constructively builds resilience, preparing you to navigate future challenges with composure. As you continue to engage with your audience and make improvements, your reputation as an adaptable and committed leader will only grow stronger.

Example: After criticism about decision-making transparency, an executive could introduce regular updates to their team or stakeholders, emphasizing openness in future communications and reinforcing trust.

LEVERAGING POSITIVE TESTIMONIALS AND BUILDING TRUST

Positive testimonials and endorsements from peers, clients, and employees are powerful tools to reinforce your reputation. By actively highlighting these endorsements, you can build trust with your audience and enhance credibility in your industry.

1. REQUEST TESTIMONIALS FROM COLLEAGUES AND CLIENTS

- **Ask for Specific Testimonials**: When requesting testimonials, ask colleagues or clients to focus on specific strengths or achievements. This provides more substance and authenticity than generic praise.
- **Incorporate Testimonials into Profiles and Presentations**: Display positive testimonials on your LinkedIn profile, personal website, and even in presentations or pitch materials. This reinforces your reputation and provides social proof of your expertise.
- **Express Appreciation**: Show gratitude to those who provide positive testimonials through public acknowledgment or private notes. Recognizing their support strengthens your professional relationships.

Example: After completing a major project, an executive could ask the client for a testimonial highlighting how their leadership and problem-solving contributed to the project's success.

2. SHARE SUCCESS STORIES AND CASE STUDIES

- **Highlight Tangible Outcomes**: Share success stories that demonstrate your expertise and the positive impact of your work. Case studies showcasing specific outcomes can be shared on your website, in articles, or during presentations to illustrate your value.
- **Use Data to Support Claims**: Include data or statistics to quantify the results. This enhances credibility by providing concrete evidence of your contributions.
- **Make Stories Relatable**: Focus on the problem, solution, and outcome to make success stories more relatable. A compelling narrative helps your audience connect with your experiences and see the practical benefits of your expertise.

Example: An executive could create a case study detailing a strategic initiative that resulted in a 30% increase in productivity, sharing the story in an article or on their LinkedIn profile to showcase their impact.

3. AMPLIFY POSITIVE MENTIONS AND REVIEWS

- **Share Positive Mentions on Social Media**: When someone praises you or your work, share their post with a thank-you note on your social media platforms. This amplifies the testimonial, reaching a wider audience and reinforcing your reputation.
- **Incorporate Reviews in Marketing Materials**: Highlight positive reviews or endorsements in marketing materials, presentations, and your personal website. This adds credibility to your brand and gives prospective clients or partners a reason to trust you.
- **Celebrate Successes Publicly**: When you or your team achieve milestones, share the news. Celebrating successes, especially those tied to customer satisfaction or impactful projects, enhances your reputation and reinforces your commitment to excellence.

Example: If a client tags an executive in a LinkedIn post praising their recent collaboration, the executive could reshare it, adding a personal note of gratitude and emphasizing their dedication to client success.

Reputation management is a continuous process that requires proactive monitoring, effective responses to feedback, and a commitment to integrity. Executives can sustain a strong brand image that builds trust and credibility by regularly assessing feedback, addressing criticism constructively, and showcasing positive testimonials. Managing your reputation reinforces your personal brand and enhances your influence as a leader, attracting opportunities and solidifying your position within your industry. Through thoughtful reputation management, you can maintain a brand that consistently reflects your values, expertise, and dedication to growth.

LEVERAGING A GOOGLE KNOWLEDGE PANEL FOR EXECUTIVE BRANDING AND REPUTATION MANAGEMENT

A Google Knowledge Panel is crucial for executives looking to manage their reputation and boost brand visibility. It provides an authoritative snapshot of your career, accomplishments, and professional identity, appearing prominently in Google search results. This section highlights the significance of Knowledge Panels in reputation management, their benefits, and steps to qualify and maintain one.

WHY A GOOGLE KNOWLEDGE PANEL MATTERS FOR EXECUTIVES

For executives, a Knowledge Panel is more than just a digital "business card." It consolidates your professional information into a visible profile, establishing a trustworthy reference point for people looking you up. Here's why it's valuable:

- **Establishes Authority and Credibility**: Google's Knowledge Panel is seen as a sign of credibility and authority. When people search for your name, the Knowledge Panel's presence signals that you are a recognized figure in your field, bolstering your reputation.
- **Enhances Brand Control**: The Knowledge Panel pulls from authoritative sources, which means that if you have a well-maintained online presence, you're likely to have control over the information displayed. This reduces the risk of misleading or inaccurate information overshadowing your professional identity.
- **Increases Visibility**: Appearing in a Knowledge Panel places you at the top of Google search results, making it easier for journalists, potential partners, clients, and employees to find reliable information about you. This increased visibility can lead to more media coverage, speaking invitations, and collaboration opportunities.

- **Reinforces Consistency Across Platforms:** Knowledge Panels typically pull data from sources such as Wikipedia, LinkedIn, and company websites. By ensuring your profiles are consistent and complete, you reinforce your brand message across multiple platforms.

BENEFITS OF A GOOGLE KNOWLEDGE PANEL FOR REPUTATION MANAGEMENT

Knowledge Panels contribute directly to reputation management by offering a concise, consistent profile of your professional life. Key benefits include:

- **Maintains Accuracy:** The information in your Knowledge Panel is sourced from verified platforms, providing accurate details about your career, achievements, and affiliations. This consistency helps prevent misinformation.
- **Reinforces Trustworthiness:** By summarizing your qualifications and experience professionally, the Knowledge Panel reassures viewers that you are a credible and authoritative figure in your industry.
- **Quickly Communicates Expertise:** A Knowledge Panel highlights key elements of your professional background—such as your title, notable achievements, and areas of expertise—enabling people to understand your qualifications and relevance quickly.
- **Showcases Positive Media Mentions:** If your Knowledge Panel includes links to reputable articles or interviews, it highlights positive media coverage, reinforcing your reputation and adding credibility.

STEPS TO QUALIFY FOR AND OPTIMIZE YOUR GOOGLE KNOWLEDGE PANEL

While Google ultimately decides who qualifies for a Knowledge Panel, there are steps you can take to increase your chances of obtaining one and maintaining its accuracy.

1. BUILD A STRONG ONLINE PRESENCE

- **Maintain Updated Social Profiles**: Ensure your LinkedIn, Twitter, and other professional profiles are fully completed and frequently updated. LinkedIn, in particular, is often cited as a source in Knowledge Panels.
- **Secure a Wikipedia Page**: Knowledge Panels frequently pull information from Wikipedia, so if you or your organization has a Wikipedia page, ensure it is well-documented, accurately sourced, and often updated.
- **Create a Personal Website**: A personal website is an authoritative source for your professional details and accomplishments. Include an "About" section with your bio, work history, publications, media appearances, and notable achievements.
- **Add Authoritative Media Mentions**: Write guest articles for reputable publications or contribute to industry journals and media outlets. Google considers verified media mentions as credible sources, which can strengthen your case for a Knowledge Panel.

Example: An executive who frequently speaks at conferences and has written for industry publications like Forbes, Inc., or Entrepreneur increases their chances of qualifying for a Knowledge Panel. Their profiles on LinkedIn and Wikipedia, as well as mentions in these reputable media sources, create a robust online footprint that Google can reference.

2. OPTIMIZE FOR SEARCH ENGINE RELEVANCE

- **Use Consistent Naming:** Use the same name format across all platforms (e.g., "Martin Rowinski, CEO of Boardsi"). This consistency helps Google associate the various sources with your identity.
- **Ensure Accurate Job Titles and Affiliations:** Ensure your current role, company affiliation, and industry-specific keywords are consistent across platforms. Using keywords that align with your expertise (e.g., "executive recruitment" or "digital transformation") enhances the likelihood of a Knowledge Panel.
- **Include Structured Data on Your Website:** If you have a personal website, implementing structured data (schema markup) can help Google better understand and display your information. This markup organizes details such as name, job title, company, and social profiles in a way that Google's algorithm can easily interpret.

Example: An executive with a personal website might use structured data to mark up their name, job title, and bio, allowing Google to recognize this content as key information for the Knowledge Panel.

3. ESTABLISH AUTHORITY THROUGH REPUTABLE CITATIONS

- **Publish Articles or Be Quoted in Industry Publications:** Being cited in major publications adds credibility to your digital footprint. Aim for mentions in respected media outlets, industry blogs, or journals regularly covering your field.
- **Engage in Public Speaking and Media Appearances:** Keynote presentations, panels, and interviews with reputable media outlets establish authority and increase online visibility. Share these appearances on your social profiles and personal websites to reinforce your brand.

- **Obtain Verified Social Media Accounts**: Verified accounts on LinkedIn or Twitter signal authenticity, which can support Google's algorithm in associating the correct information with your identity.

Example: If an executive is frequently quoted in top media outlets like the Wall Street Journal or Bloomberg, these citations reinforce their authority and provide high-quality links that Google can use as sources for their Knowledge Panel.

4. MONITOR AND MAINTAIN YOUR KNOWLEDGE PANEL

Once a Knowledge Panel is established, keeping your information accurate and up-to-date is essential to sustain your credibility.

- **Suggest Edits to Google**: If your Knowledge Panel contains incorrect information, you can suggest edits directly through Google. Use this feature to keep your profile accurate and reflect your current achievements.
- **Update Key Profiles Regularly**: Regularly update your LinkedIn, Wikipedia, and personal website to ensure consistency. Any major achievements, new roles, or noteworthy media mentions should be added promptly.
- **Encourage Positive Mentions and Media Engagement**: Actively seek out media opportunities, such as interviews and guest articles, to continue building your brand and adding new, authoritative sources for Google to reference.

Example: An executive who recently received an industry award can update their LinkedIn, personal website, and Wikipedia page with this information. They can also encourage media mentions by sharing the news through press releases or interviews, further reinforcing their credibility.

MAKING THE MOST OF YOUR GOOGLE KNOWLEDGE PANEL

Once your Knowledge Panel is established, it becomes a highly visible, trust-building asset. Here are some ways to leverage it effectively:

- **Direct Prospective Partners or Clients to Your Panel**: When connecting with new stakeholders, suggest they Google your name. The Knowledge Panel provides them with verified, relevant information about you, establishing credibility and authority immediately.
- **Use the Panel as a Marketing Tool**: Highlight your Knowledge Panel as a testament to your influence in your field. For instance, in networking events or conferences, encourage attendees to look up your Knowledge Panel to learn more about your accomplishments.
- **Incorporate the Panel into Brand-Building Activities**: The Knowledge Panel can be valuable to brand-building materials, such as investor presentations or pitch decks. Including it as a reference point reinforces your brand authority.

Example: An executive speaking at a conference might mention they have a Knowledge Panel and invite attendees to search for them on Google. This allows the audience to access a verified source of information, enhancing the executive's perceived credibility.

A Google Knowledge Panel is a valuable asset for executives looking to boost their online reputation and brand credibility. By strategically building a strong online presence, ensuring accurate and consistent information, and engaging in media activities that reinforce your authority, you can increase your chances of securing a Knowledge Panel. Once established, this digital profile serves as a central, visible hub for your professional identity, fostering trust and confidence in your leadership. As part of a comprehensive reputation management strategy, a Knowledge Panel solidifies your position as a respected thought leader in your industry, further supporting your ongoing brand-building efforts.

UNLOCK THE MAGIC—
SCAN, TO LEARN MORE!

NAVIGATING CHALLENGES AND CRISIS MANAGEMENT

In an executive's career, challenges are inevitable, and how these challenges are managed can define or even redefine one's professional trajectory. During times of crisis—whether it's a public relations debacle, an operational setback, or a significant industry disruption—leaders are expected to navigate uncertainty while safeguarding their brand's integrity. Effective crisis management goes beyond mere damage control; it is an opportunity to demonstrate resilience, transparency, and ethical leadership. This chapter explores strategies for managing crises while preserving brand integrity, drawing lessons from real-life case studies of executives who successfully handled difficult situations.

While every executive would ideally avoid facing a crisis that tests their brand and reputation, challenges and unexpected setbacks are almost unavoidable in the fast-paced world of business. Though we hope you'll never need to reference this chapter, preparing for potential crises is essential to safeguarding your brand's integrity. Effective crisis management isn't about anticipating the worst; rather, it's about being ready to face challenges with resilience, transparency, and a steady hand when they arise. This chapter provides you with the tools to handle difficult situations strategically and gracefully, ensuring that if a crisis does occur, you can transform it into an opportunity for growth and reinforce trust with those around you.

WHY CRISIS MANAGEMENT MATTERS FOR EXECUTIVES

For executives, the way a crisis is handled can have a profound and lasting impact on both personal and organizational reputations. A well-managed crisis response can actually enhance trust, loyalty, and credibility among stakeholders, while a poorly handled crisis can lead to significant damage, eroding confidence and relationships. Crisis management is a vital skill for executives—not only for solving immediate problems but also for showcasing resilience, transparency, and leadership integrity. Here's why mastering crisis management is crucial for executives and how it contributes to long-term success.

PROTECTS BRAND INTEGRITY

During a crisis, executives are often thrust into the spotlight, with the public, media, and stakeholders closely watching their every move. A crisis response that aligns with your core values and reinforces brand integrity can strengthen your reputation as a principled, trustworthy leader. How you react to difficult situations reveals your commitment to these values, demonstrating that they are not just words on paper, but guiding principles that inform your actions, even under pressure. On the other hand, evasive or self-serving actions can damage your credibility and raise doubts about your leadership. By responding in ways that honor your brand values, you protect your reputation and send a clear signal that you are a leader of integrity.

BUILDS TRUST AND TRANSPARENCY

Transparency and responsiveness during a crisis are critical for maintaining trust with stakeholders. Addressing issues openly and effectively communicating your actions and intentions can reassure clients, employees, investors, and partners that you are reliable. When stakeholders see that you're willing to confront challenges head-on, admit mistakes, and keep them informed, they feel valued and are more likely to remain supportive. A transparent approach fosters loyalty, showing that you prioritize ethical behavior and accountability. This builds a strong foundation of trust that will benefit both you and your organization, whether in calm or turbulent times.

PROVIDES OPPORTUNITIES FOR GROWTH

Every crisis presents an opportunity to learn and grow. Confronting challenges directly enables executives to identify underlying issues, pinpoint areas for improvement, and implement new strategies or policies. This proactive approach to learning from adversity strengthens a growth-oriented mindset, showing that you view challenges as opportunities for progress rather than setbacks. By transforming crises into catalysts for positive change, you not only enhance your organization's resilience but also reinforce your personal brand as a forward-thinking, adaptable leader who can turn difficult situations into meaningful advancements.

STRENGTHENS STAKEHOLDER LOYALTY

Managing crises with confidence and skill can deepen loyalty among employees, clients, and investors, who respect leaders who remain composed under pressure. Demonstrating resilience, empathy, and decisiveness during difficult times shows stakeholders that you are equipped to guide them through adversity. When people see a leader committed to solving problems and supporting those affected, they are more likely to stand by that leader in the future. This loyalty is particularly valuable during recovery periods, as it fosters a unified, motivated environment where everyone feels they are part of a team led by someone capable and trustworthy.

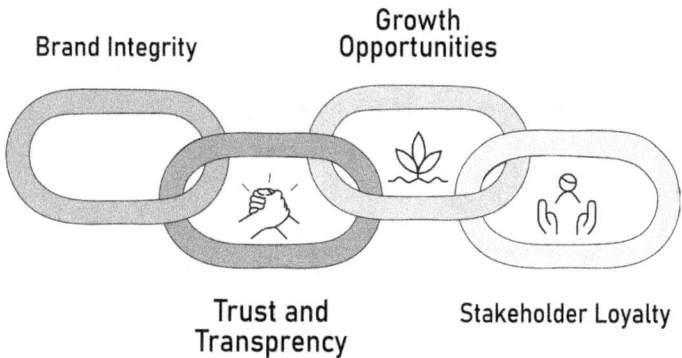

For executives, effective crisis management is more than just resolving an issue; it's an opportunity to reinforce brand integrity, build trust, embrace growth, and foster stakeholder loyalty. By mastering the art of handling crises with transparency, resilience, and a commitment to improvement, you not only navigate immediate challenges but also enhance your long-term reputation as a principled and capable leader.

PROACTIVE CRISIS MANAGEMENT STRATEGIES

Effective crisis management begins long before a problem arises. By preparing in advance, you can act quickly, minimize damage, and confidently handle unexpected events.

1. DEVELOP A CRISIS MANAGEMENT PLAN

- **Identify Potential Crisis Scenarios**: Assess areas within your industry or organization that could pose potential risks. These could include data breaches, operational failures, regulatory changes, or

employee-related incidents. Anticipating potential crises enables you to prepare specific response strategies.
- **Establish a Crisis Response Team**: Designate a team of trusted advisors or colleagues to assist with decision-making and communication during a crisis. This team should include key roles, such as public relations, legal, and department heads, to ensure comprehensive coverage of all aspects of the crisis.
- **Define Clear Roles and Responsibilities**: Each crisis team member should understand their role and responsibility, from drafting official statements to communicating with stakeholders. A clear chain of command ensures swift, organized responses.

Example: An executive at a technology firm might prepare a crisis plan for potential data breaches, outlining specific roles for the IT, PR, and customer service teams. This plan would include steps for securing data, notifying affected customers, and managing public communication.

2. ESTABLISH CORE PRINCIPLES FOR CRISIS COMMUNICATION

- **Prioritize Transparency**: During a crisis, transparency is essential for maintaining credibility. Be honest about what has occurred, what steps are being taken to address it, and what affected parties can expect.
- **Emphasize Accountability**: If the crisis is due to an internal error, acknowledge the mistake. Demonstrating accountability shows integrity and builds trust, especially if the response includes corrective measures.
- **Be Consistent in Messaging**: Consistency across all communication channels (emails, social media, press releases) helps prevent misunderstandings. Work closely with your PR and communication teams to ensure that messages align with your brand's core values and address concerns accurately.

Example: When a prominent executive at a retail company faced backlash over a product recall, their team issued consistent messaging across social media, press releases, and customer emails. They apologized for the oversight, took responsibility, and provided information on product returns and refunds, maintaining transparency throughout the process.

3. PREPARE YOUR PUBLIC STATEMENT IN ADVANCE

- **Craft a Template for Rapid Response**: In a crisis, time is of the essence. Having a templated response ready allows you to address the public quickly while refining specific details as the situation unfolds.
- **Address Key Concerns Directly**: A public statement should address the primary issues immediately, including what happened, who is affected, and what actions are being taken. Anticipate audience concerns and respond to them directly within the statement.
- **Emphasize Positive Actions**: Outline any steps you're taking to resolve the issue and prevent recurrence. If appropriate, express empathy toward those affected to demonstrate that you understand the impact.

Example: In the case of a manufacturing error, an executive's public statement might begin with an apology, briefly explain the error, and then outline the steps to correct it. By addressing the situation directly and providing solutions, they reaffirm their commitment to quality and accountability.

RESPONDING TO THE CRISIS IN REAL-TIME

Once a crisis emerges, it's essential to remain calm, act swiftly, and stay aligned with your principles and brand image. Here are real-time strategies to handle a crisis, reinforcing integrity and trust.

1. MAINTAIN OPEN LINES OF COMMUNICATION

- **Be Available and Accessible**: Ensure your team, stakeholders, and the public access updates. This might include holding a press conference, sending regular email updates, or hosting virtual town hall meetings to provide real-time information.
- **Engage on Social Media**: Social media platforms allow for direct, immediate communication with your audience. Use these channels to post updates, respond to inquiries, and address concerns as the situation evolves.
- **Provide a Single Source of Truth**: Use one central hub (such as your website or a dedicated crisis page) where stakeholders can access all official updates, FAQs, and next steps. This reduces confusion and ensures everyone receives the same accurate information.

Example: A hospitality executive facing a crisis related to a health outbreak might use social media to post regular updates on precautionary measures and link to a webpage with detailed information and safety procedures.

2. MONITOR PUBLIC PERCEPTION AND RESPOND APPROPRIATELY

- **Use Monitoring Tools**: Social listening tools like Mention or Brandwatch can track how people react to crises and identify common questions or concerns. Staying aware of public sentiment allows you to adjust your messaging if needed.
- **Acknowledge Misunderstandings Quickly**: If misinformation spreads, address it directly and clarify the facts. Doing so promptly minimizes damage and reestablishes control over the narrative.
- **Respond to Feedback with Empathy**: If customers, employees, or partners express frustration, respond empathetically and acknowledge their concerns. Show that you understand their position and provide additional support where possible.

Example: An executive facing negative press might notice recurring customer concerns about response times. In response, they could issue a public apology for delays and explain steps being taken to expedite support.

3. STAY ADAPTABLE AND MAKE DATA-DRIVEN ADJUSTMENTS

- **Be Ready to Pivot**: Crises are dynamic, and new information may require changes in your response plan. Stay flexible, adjusting your approach while remaining true to your values and maintaining transparency.
- **Use Real-Time Data**: Monitor data from customer feedback, media coverage, and social media analytics to gauge response effectiveness. If certain actions aren't resonating well, adjust your approach based on the data.
- **Prepare for Long-Term Recovery**: Some crises, especially reputation damage, may require long-term effort to rebuild trust. Outline a recovery plan that includes continuous engagement and proactive improvements.

Example: If an initial statement is poorly received, an executive might adjust their messaging in follow-up statements, addressing specific concerns raised by stakeholders to show responsiveness and adaptability.

LEARNING FROM REAL-LIFE CASE STUDIES

Learning from other executives who successfully managed crises can provide valuable insights and practical strategies. Here are two notable examples:

CASE STUDY 1: JOHNSON & JOHNSON'S TYLENOL CRISIS

In 1982, Johnson & Johnson faced a major crisis when seven people died after ingesting cyanide-laced Tylenol capsules. Despite the product tampering being beyond the company's control, Johnson & Johnson prioritized consumer safety over profits by issuing a nationwide recall and halting production, costing the company millions.

Key Takeaways:

- **Prioritize Safety and Trust**: Johnson & Johnson's swift action showed that they valued customer safety above financial considerations, which helped them rebuild trust.
- **Be Transparent and Proactive**: The company provided regular updates and worked with law enforcement, demonstrating transparency and accountability.
- **Reinforce with Long-Term Solutions**: Johnson & Johnson introduced tamper-proof packaging, setting a new industry safety standard, and reinforcing their commitment to consumer protection.

CASE STUDY 2: STARBUCKS' RESPONSE TO RACIAL BIAS INCIDENT

In 2018, Starbucks faced backlash after an incident in Philadelphia where two Black men were arrested while waiting in a store without making a purchase. In response, Starbucks' CEO, Kevin Johnson, issued a public apology, closed over 8,000 stores for racial bias training, and worked to address issues of inclusivity within the organization.

Key Takeaways:

- **Address the Issue Head-On**: Starbucks responded quickly, acknowledging the issue and taking responsibility, which helped mitigate public outrage.

- **Take Meaningful Action**: By implementing company-wide bias training, Starbucks demonstrated a genuine commitment to change, showing they took the incident seriously.
- **Use Crises as Learning Opportunities**: Starbucks' response transformed a negative event into an opportunity to foster inclusivity and set an example for other corporations.

TURNING CRISES INTO OPPORTUNITIES FOR POSITIVE CHANGE

While crises are challenging, they offer a unique opportunity to reinforce your brand's values and commitment to integrity. By using a proactive approach to crisis management, you can turn a difficult situation into a chance to demonstrate resilience, ethical leadership, and dedication to improvement.

1. PUBLICLY COMMIT TO LONG-TERM IMPROVEMENTS

- **Outline Clear Next Steps**: After the initial crisis response, share a long-term plan that addresses root causes and prevents similar incidents in the future.
- **Engage Stakeholders in Recovery Efforts**: Invite stakeholders to provide input on changes, showing that you value their perspective and are committed to transparency.
- **Communicate Progress Regularly**: Continue to update stakeholders on progress toward improvements, reinforcing your commitment to positive change.

Example: An executive at a tech company might establish a series of employee workshops on ethical data usage following a data privacy incident, sharing updates on workshop outcomes and any resulting policy changes.

2. REINFORCE CORE VALUES DURING RECOVERY

- **Reconnect with Your Brand's Mission**: During recovery, use messaging that emphasizes your brand's core mission and values, helping to restore faith in your commitment to integrity.
- **Show Empathy and Support**: Demonstrate care and empathy, especially for those directly impacted by the crisis. Personalizing your response shows stakeholders that you genuinely care about their experience.
- **Celebrate Milestones in Recovery**: Recognize and celebrate milestones, such as implementing new policies or completing an employee training program, to reinforce positive progress and keep stakeholders engaged.

Example: If an executive faced a crisis related to workplace culture, they could implement initiatives to improve employee well-being and recognize progress by celebrating employee feedback and new support programs.

Navigating challenges and managing crises are essential skills for executives aiming to sustain brand integrity and build a resilient reputation. By proactively preparing, responding with transparency and empathy, and drawing lessons from past experiences, executives can transform crises into opportunities for growth and positive change. When addressed thoughtfully, crises become defining moments that highlight your leadership, reinforce your values, and demonstrate a steadfast commitment to ethical principles. Ultimately, these moments strengthen your reputation as a trusted and effective leader.

UNLOCK THE MAGIC— SCAN, TO LEARN MORE!

11

MEASURING YOUR EXECUTIVE BRAND IMPACT

Building a strong executive brand is a strategic endeavor that requires ongoing evaluation to ensure its effectiveness and alignment with your goals. Measuring the impact of your executive brand enables you to assess what's working, identify areas for improvement, and refine your approach using actionable data. By tracking specific metrics and leveraging powerful tools, you gain valuable insights into your brand's visibility, engagement, and influence on your career progression.

In this chapter, we'll explore the key metrics and tools for measuring your executive brand's impact, ranging from social media analytics to personal growth milestones. Understanding these indicators will equip you to make data-driven decisions that amplify your brand's reach and enhance its influence in meaningful ways.

WHY MEASURING YOUR BRAND IMPACT IS ESSENTIAL

Measuring your brand's impact isn't just about checking boxes or tracking vanity metrics. It's a strategic practice that enables you to fully harness the power of your executive brand. For executives, a well-managed brand goes beyond mere visibility or presence—it's a strategic asset that opens doors to career opportunities, leadership roles, and greater credibility and authority within your industry. In today's competitive professional landscape, where reputations are shaped by perception as much as by accomplishments, understanding your brand's real impact is crucial.

Tracking your brand's impact informs your strategy, revealing where your brand resonates most and where it may need refinement. Without measurable insights, branding efforts risk being guided by assumptions rather than data, leading to missed opportunities or misaligned messaging. Metrics provide clarity on how effectively your brand aligns with audience expectations, which messages connect most powerfully, and which platforms yield the highest engagement. This feedback loop allows you to make informed adjustments, ensuring that each effort enhances your presence and reinforces your authority.

In addition to shaping your strategy, measuring brand impact demonstrates the return on investment (ROI) of your efforts. Executive branding requires significant investments of time, energy, and often financial resources—whether through content creation, public speaking, networking, or media appearances. By tracking outcomes such as increased visibility, new career opportunities, or heightened engagement, you can showcase tangible results. These metrics not only validate your efforts but also communicate their value to stakeholders who may support or benefit from your branding initiatives. By converting intangible assets—like reputation and influence—into measurable achievements, ROI metrics prove that your branding efforts deliver meaningful results.

Regularly evaluating your brand's impact also ensures that it remains aligned with your career goals and adapts to evolving industry trends. Personal branding isn't a one-time project; it's a dynamic process that evolves alongside your professional growth. As you advance in your career, move into new areas of influence, or shift your focus, your brand should reflect these changes. Metrics enable you to assess whether your brand stays relevant to your goals or if adjustments are necessary to better align with your current trajectory. This adaptability helps maintain relevance and prevents stagnation.

Unveiling the Dimensions of Executive Brand Impact

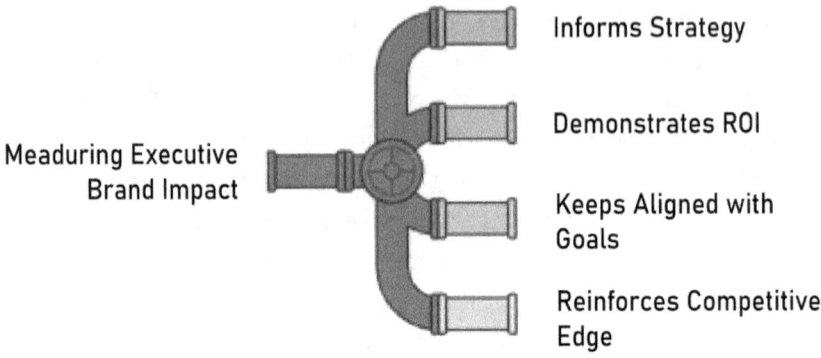

Embracing a data-driven approach to brand management solidifies your competitive advantage. By prioritizing initiatives that enhance your reputation, distinguish your insights, and amplify your thought leadership, you become more prominent in the eyes of peers, clients, and industry leaders. A brand rooted in data adapts continuously to better serve its audience, fostering greater engagement and trust. With measurable insights guiding your strategy, you can craft a distinct, impactful executive brand that reflects your current expertise while positioning you for future growth and influence.

KEY METRICS FOR MEASURING EXECUTIVE BRAND IMPACT

The impact of an executive brand can be evaluated across multiple dimensions, ranging from visibility and engagement to tangible career achievements. Below are the key metrics to monitor:

1. BRAND VISIBILITY AND REACH

Brand visibility and reach are the cornerstones of any successful executive branding strategy. These metrics reveal how many people are aware of your brand and how far your message extends across platforms and audiences. Visibility provides a snapshot of your brand's current standing, while reach measures how effectively your content resonates and spreads. Together, they offer critical insights into your brand's perception and influence within your industry.

A primary indicator of brand visibility is your social media following and connections, particularly on platforms like LinkedIn, Twitter, and Instagram, where professional engagement thrives. Tracking the growth of your followers and network reveals how well your brand resonates with your audience. A steady increase in followers indicates relevance and growing appreciation for your expertise. Executives who regularly share thought leadership content—such as articles, insights, or industry updates—often see a marked rise in their follower count, reflecting an expanding presence and greater content engagement.

Website traffic is another vital metric for assessing visibility and reach. Tools like Google Analytics allow you to monitor the number of visitors, page views, and time spent on key sections of your site. Analyzing these metrics reveals audience interest in your content and helps identify the types of content that resonate most. Spikes in traffic after publishing specific posts, for instance, signal strong audience alignment with those topics. Additionally, understanding traffic sources—be it social media, search engines, or direct referrals—can guide strategic decisions on where to focus branding efforts.

Search volume for your name and related keywords provides further insight into brand awareness. An increase in searches indicates growing interest and visibility. Securing a Google Knowledge Panel can further enhance your brand's reach and credibility by centralizing key information in one authoritative location. This not only consolidates your digital presence but also ensures accuracy and consistency in how you are perceived.

For example, an executive who observes a 20% increase in LinkedIn followers over a quarter after consistently sharing thought leadership content demonstrates growing visibility. This growth reflects the value of their insights, while shares and engagements amplify their brand's reach. By carefully tracking metrics across social media, website traffic, and search trends, you can continuously evaluate and refine your brand's visibility, ensuring maximum impact.

2. ENGAGEMENT AND INTERACTION

Engagement and interaction are critical measures of how effectively your content resonates with your audience. While visibility metrics highlight how many people encounter your brand, engagement metrics delve into the quality of those interactions. High engagement signifies that your message not only reaches your audience but also inspires dialogue, interest, and action. For executives, it reflects the relevance of your insights, the value of your ideas, and your growing influence within your network.

Social media metrics, such as likes, comments, and shares, offer straightforward indicators of engagement. These metrics reveal how your audience responds to your content—whether they find it valuable, thought-provoking, or insightful. High engagement on LinkedIn posts, Twitter updates, and Instagram stories suggests that your content resonates strongly. Comments, in particular, signify deeper connections, as they require effort and indicate that your audience is actively participating in the conversation.

Click-through rates (CTR) provide additional insight into engagement by measuring the percentage of people who interact with links in your posts, such as articles, videos, or website resources. High CTRs demonstrate that your content is compelling and drives audience action, whether through further exploration or deeper engagement. For executives, a high CTR often translates to meaningful interactions, as your audience actively seeks to engage with the resources and insights you share.

Direct messages and inquiries are another valuable layer of engagement. These interactions reflect the trust and credibility your brand has established, prompting individuals to reach out for questions, feedback, or potential collaborations. For executives, such messages indicate that your brand not only engages but also builds authority and fosters meaningful connections. Regular inquiries or collaboration requests suggest growing influence and recognition as a trusted resource and partner.

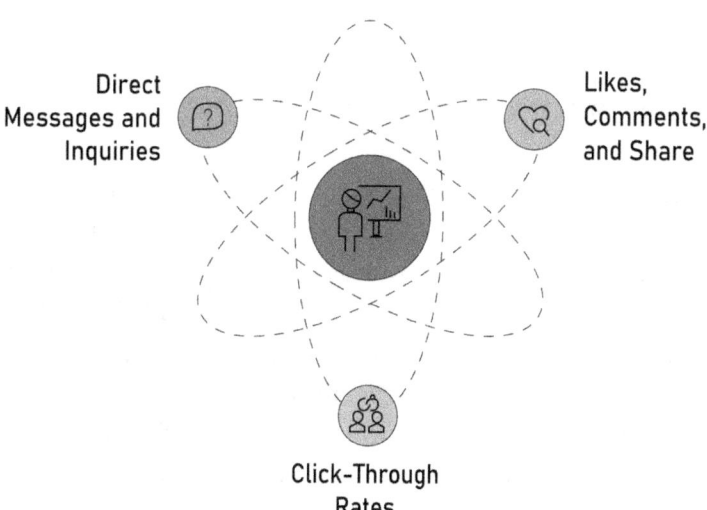

Measuring Executive Brand Impact

If you post a thought leadership article on LinkedIn and it garners 100 comments and 50 shares, it demonstrates a high level of engagement. This kind of interaction indicates that your content resonates deeply with your professional network, sparking conversation and generating broader interest as it's shared across connections. Such engagement not only boosts your visibility but also solidifies your reputation as a thought leader offering meaningful insights. By closely monitoring metrics like social media interactions, click-through rates (CTR), and direct inquiries, you gain a clearer understanding of how your audience connects with your brand. This insight allows you to refine your content strategy, fostering even stronger connections.

3. CONTENT PERFORMANCE AND INFLUENCE

Analyzing the performance of your content provides valuable insights into what resonates with your audience, helping you enhance your influence as an executive. By monitoring metrics such as engagement, shares, and sentiment, you can identify the topics and formats that are most effective. This data-driven approach enables you to refine your content strategy, amplify your reach, and establish yourself as a credible leader. Here's how tracking content metrics can help you shape an influential brand:

TOP-PERFORMING CONTENT

Identifying your top-performing content—whether it's an article, social media post, video, or webinar—gives you a clear view of what generates the highest engagement. By analyzing pieces that receive the most views, likes, comments, or shares, you can uncover patterns that reflect your audience's preferences. This information informs future content creation, allowing you to prioritize topics that resonate most with your followers. For instance, if a post about innovation strategies performs exceptionally well, you might develop a series on related themes, reinforcing your expertise and deepening audience engagement.

CONTENT SHARES AND BACKLINKS

Content that is widely shared or linked by others is a powerful indicator of influence. Monitoring the frequency of shares and tracking backlinks from reputable sites extends your reach to new audiences while enhancing your credibility. Shares signal that your content is valuable enough to be recommended by others, while backlinks from trusted sources bolster your authority. Additionally, these metrics improve your visibility in search engine results, driving organic traffic. For example, an article shared by a leading industry publication or linked on influential blogs positions you as a respected thought leader within your field.

SENTIMENT ANALYSIS

Understanding the sentiment behind responses to your content offers a nuanced perspective on how your brand is perceived. Sentiment analysis tools, such as Brandwatch or Mention, help assess whether comments and mentions are positive, neutral, or negative. Positive sentiment indicates that your messaging resonates, while neutral or negative feedback provides opportunities for improvement. By analyzing sentiment, you can fine-tune your tone or approach. For instance, if an article on crisis management receives feedback highlighting concerns or misunderstandings, you can address these insights in future content to build trust and credibility.

Tracking metrics like top-performing posts, shares, backlinks, and sentiment analysis allows you to refine your strategy, expand your reach, and enhance your influence. By focusing on topics that resonate, monitoring content dissemination, and understanding audience feedback, you create a feedback loop that continuously improves your brand's relevance and impact. This data-driven approach positions you as a responsive, influential leader, attuned to your audience's needs and committed to delivering valuable insights.

4. CAREER PROGRESSION AND PROFESSIONAL IMPACT

The ultimate goal of your executive brand is to support your career growth, expand your influence, and open pathways to new opportunities. Monitoring the impact of your branding efforts on career progression provides valuable insights into the return on investment for the time and resources you dedicate to building your professional presence. A strong brand not only enhances your visibility but also positions you as a sought-after leader. Key indicators to assess the effectiveness of your branding include:

NEW OPPORTUNITIES

An increase in career advancements and opportunities—such as job offers, board invitations, speaking engagements, or consulting requests—indicates that your executive brand is gaining traction. These opportunities signal that your expertise is valued and your brand resonates within your industry. Tracking these developments over time helps gauge whether your branding efforts are reaching the right audience. For instance, frequent invitations to speak at industry events demonstrate that your insights are recognized, allowing you to expand your influence and solidify your position as a thought leader.

INDUSTRY RECOGNITION AND AWARDS

Recognition through industry awards, nominations, or positive media mentions validates the impact of your brand. These accolades highlight your credibility and expertise, signaling that your contributions are respected within your field. Awards and media coverage can also attract further opportunities and partnerships, creating a virtuous cycle of visibility and influence. Highlighting these achievements in your professional profiles amplifies their impact, reinforcing your alignment with excellence and leadership.

PARTNERSHIPS AND COLLABORATIONS

Successful branding often leads to partnerships and collaborations with other respected professionals or organizations. Note any partnerships resulting from your branding efforts, as these are often built on shared values and mutual recognition of expertise. Collaborations—such as joint projects, co-authored articles, or strategic alliances—demonstrate that others trust and value your leadership. For example, being approached by a well-known company for a consulting project or joint initiative underscores your reputation as a go-to expert in your field.

By tracking career advancements, industry recognition, and new partnerships, you gain a comprehensive view of your brand's effectiveness. Each opportunity, award, or collaboration reflects the reach and credibility of your efforts, demonstrating that your brand opens doors, attracts recognition, and builds a robust network of influence. As you continue to refine your strategy, these indicators ensure your executive brand remains a valuable asset in your ongoing career progression and professional impact.

TOOLS FOR MEASURING BRAND IMPACT

There are various tools available to help executives measure their branding effectiveness. These tools can track social media engagement, analyze website traffic, and provide insights into content performance.

1. SOCIAL MEDIA ANALYTICS TOOLS

- **LinkedIn Analytics**: LinkedIn provides metrics on profile views, post impressions, and engagement rates, giving insights into how well your content resonates with your professional network.
- **Twitter Analytics**: Twitter's built-in analytics tool allows you to monitor tweet impressions, engagement rates, and follower growth, helping to measure brand visibility and engagement on the platform.

- **Instagram Insights**: If you use Instagram for professional branding, Instagram Insights offers data on reach, profile visits, follower demographics, and post interactions.

Example: After running a campaign on LinkedIn, an executive could analyze post impressions, engagement, and new followers to gauge how effectively their content reached and resonated with their target audience.

2. GOOGLE ANALYTICS

- **Traffic Sources and Behavior Flow**: Google Analytics helps track traffic sources, showing how people found your site (e.g., direct, referral, social) and which content they engaged with most.
- **Audience Demographics**: Google Analytics provides data on your audience's demographics, including age, gender, and location, allowing you to tailor future content to suit their preferences better.
- **Conversions and Goals**: Set specific goals (e.g., newsletter sign-ups and contact form submissions) to track how well your website drives action, giving you insights into its effectiveness in building engagement.

Example: An executive could use Google Analytics to monitor the success of a newly launched blog. If certain articles attract high traffic, they can focus future content on similar topics.

3. MEDIA MONITORING AND SENTIMENT ANALYSIS TOOLS

- **Mention and Brandwatch**: These tools track mentions of your name, brand, or specific keywords across social media and the web. They also offer sentiment analysis, providing a snapshot of public opinion.

- **Google Alerts**: Set up Google Alerts for your name, company, and industry keywords. This free tool notifies you of new mentions online, helping you stay aware of how your brand is discussed.

Example: If an executive is quoted in a major industry publication, media monitoring tools will alert them to the mention, allowing them to share the coverage on social media or their website.

4. CRM AND EMAIL MARKETING TOOLS

- **HubSpot and Salesforce**: CRMs like HubSpot and Salesforce allow you to track interactions with contacts, helping you understand how your brand influences networking and partnership opportunities.
- **Mailchimp and Constant Contact**: Email marketing tools provide analytics on open rates, click-through rates, and subscriber growth. This data shows how well your content is engaging your email audience.

Example: After sending out a monthly newsletter, an executive can analyze open and click-through rates to gauge interest in the topics covered, adjusting future content based on what resonates.

REFINING YOUR BRAND STRATEGY BASED ON RESULTS

Tracking metrics provides valuable insights, but the real power lies in interpreting and acting on this data to strengthen your brand. By leveraging engagement metrics, demographic data, and audience feedback, you can refine your branding strategy to maximize its impact and align it with your long-term career goals. Below is a step-by-step guide to refining your brand using data-driven insights.

1. FOCUS ON HIGH-IMPACT AREAS

Analyzing your content's performance helps identify what resonates most with your audience, allowing you to amplify popular topics, improve underperforming content, and strategically target specific audience segments.

- **Double Down on Popular Topics**: Use engagement data to pinpoint topics that consistently perform well. Prioritize future content on these high-performing areas to establish yourself as an authority in areas that matter to your audience. For instance, if posts on leadership innovation receive high engagement, consider expanding this theme with related topics to maintain interest and reinforce your expertise.
- **Adjust Underperforming Content**: When certain topics or formats fail to connect, experiment with new approaches. Enhance complex subjects with visual elements like infographics, or simplify messaging for technical content. By adapting your style and keeping content fresh, you can better engage your audience and boost relevance.
- **Target Specific Audiences**: Demographic data provides insights into your audience's roles, industries, and interests. Use this information to tailor content for specific segments. For example, if a significant portion of your audience includes emerging leaders, create content addressing their unique challenges and aspirations to deepen engagement and strengthen your connection with them.

2. SET NEW GOALS BASED ON PROGRESS

As your brand evolves, so should your objectives. Regularly updating and reviewing your goals ensures your strategy stays aligned with your career path and industry dynamics.

- **Establish New Metrics**: As your brand matures, introduce metrics that reflect growth goals, such as expanding your presence on additional platforms, increasing engagement within targeted demographics, or growing your professional network. These metrics provide measurable, attainable benchmarks that enhance your branding efforts' overall impact.

- **Regularly Review and Adjust Goals**: Branding is an ongoing journey that demands periodic reassessment. Evaluate your goals regularly and refine them based on career developments, industry trends, and audience feedback. This adaptable approach keeps your strategy agile and responsive, ensuring your efforts remain effective and aligned with your evolving objectives.

3. CELEBRATE AND SHARE SUCCESSES

Recognizing and sharing milestones enhances your credibility and reinforces your brand's impact. Highlighting achievements and positive feedback creates a compelling narrative that resonates with your audience.

- **Highlight Milestones**: Share accomplishments such as reaching follower milestones, publishing successful articles, or earning industry recognition. Celebrating these moments publicly demonstrates growth and authority. For example, if you're featured in a prominent publication, share the news to underscore your expertise and expand your visibility.
- **Leverage Testimonials and Positive Feedback**: Displaying testimonials, endorsements, or supportive comments builds trust and strengthens credibility. Incorporate these into your online profiles or share them on social media. For instance, if a respected industry leader endorses your work, share their remarks with your audience to reinforce your influence and demonstrate the value of your insights.

EXAMPLE IN ACTION

Consider an executive who successfully grew their LinkedIn following through a content series on leadership strategies. To mark this milestone, they share a post thanking their followers and inviting feedback on future topics. This not only highlights the impact of their brand but also fosters engagement and positions them as an approachable, responsive thought leader.

CONCLUSION

Measuring the impact of your branding efforts is vital to refining your approach and building a brand that truly resonates and delivers results. By tracking metrics related to visibility, engagement, content performance, and career impact, you can create a data-driven strategy that enhances your professional reputation and positions you for long-term success. With a clear understanding of what works and where adjustments are needed, you can evolve your executive brand to strengthen your influence, elevate your career, and leave a lasting legacy in your industry.

UNLOCK THE MAGIC—
SCAN, TO LEARN MORE!

12

THE ROLE OF MENTORSHIP IN EXECUTIVE BRANDING

Mentorship is a powerful yet often underutilized tool in executive branding. Both mentoring others and seeking guidance from mentors can profoundly elevate an executive's professional presence. Engaging in mentorship demonstrates leadership qualities, expands your network, and builds a reputation for generosity and expertise. For executives, embracing the dual roles of mentor and mentee fosters personal and professional growth while solidifying your brand's credibility and value in the industry.

Mentorship creates a dynamic, reciprocal relationship where both parties benefit. As a mentor, sharing your experience, knowledge, and insights supports another's growth while showcasing your expertise and leadership qualities. This form of leadership highlights your ability to guide and inspire, adding depth to your brand and signaling a commitment to developing others. Mentoring enables you to leave a lasting legacy by shaping future leaders who embody the values and skills you impart. For executives, this reinforces your image as a knowledgeable, approachable, and influential leader.

Conversely, being a mentee enriches your brand by showcasing a commitment to continuous learning and self-improvement. Seeking mentorship reflects humility and a growth-oriented mindset—traits essential for a strong executive brand. Learning from others broadens your perspective, exposes you to innovative ideas, and deepens your understanding of industry trends. Demonstrating a willingness to learn and adapt resonates with today's dynamic business environment, positioning you as a versatile and forward-thinking leader.

WHY MENTORSHIP IS ESSENTIAL FOR EXECUTIVE BRANDING

Mentorship enhances qualities that elevate your executive brand. As a mentor, you establish yourself as a leader, displaying both knowledge and generosity. As a mentee, you embody curiosity, adaptability, and a dedication to personal growth. These roles add valuable dimensions to your brand, making you a relatable and multifaceted leader.

Mentorship offers an authentic platform to showcase your leadership style. As a mentor, you lead by example, demonstrating patience, empathy, and strategic thinking. Mentees observe firsthand how you approach challenges and make decisions, cementing your reputation as a thoughtful and skilled leader. This visibility reinforces your brand in ways conventional branding efforts cannot achieve.

Similarly, being a mentee strengthens your brand by highlighting your dedication to growth. In today's business landscape, adaptability and openness to learning are highly valued. Seeking mentorship signals an understanding of continuous development, distinguishing you as an executive who prioritizes collaboration and lifelong learning.

THE BENEFITS OF MENTORSHIP IN EXPANDING YOUR PROFESSIONAL NETWORK

Mentorship unlocks new connections and broadens your professional network. As a mentor, you engage with other leaders, mentors, and professionals involved in similar initiatives. These connections create opportunities to build relationships with individuals who share your values and professional interests, increasing your visibility and influence within the industry.

Mentees also introduce fresh perspectives and connections, often connecting mentors with emerging professionals and rising talent. These interactions keep you attuned to evolving trends and skills in your field. A mentee may even introduce you to innovative tools or contemporary approaches that enhance your work. This mutually beneficial exchange strengthens your network with diverse expertise and perspectives.

As a mentee, you gain access to your mentor's network, leading to introductions with seasoned professionals who can offer guidance, collaboration opportunities, or career advancement. For executives, such access is invaluable, especially when exploring board roles, consulting positions, or senior-level opportunities. A mentor's endorsement within their network can open doors that might otherwise remain closed, amplifying your influence in the industry.

MENTORSHIP AS A SHOWCASE OF LEADERSHIP AND EXPERTISE

Mentorship provides a unique platform to demonstrate your expertise authentically and impactfully. By guiding others, you share valuable insights and help mentees navigate career challenges, positioning yourself as a trusted and knowledgeable leader in your field.

Through mentorship, you showcase your problem-solving approach, communication skills, and strategic insights, all of which reinforce your brand identity. These interactions allow stakeholders to witness your patience, adaptability, and values—traits that define effective leadership. Demonstrating qualities like integrity, transparency, and innovation reinforces the authenticity of your executive brand.

Sharing your journey, including successes and setbacks, makes you more relatable and approachable, enhancing trust and credibility. Transparency fosters an environment of openness and support, benefiting your mentees while elevating your reputation across your broader network. Colleagues and peers see you as a leader committed to sharing knowledge and nurturing talent, reinforcing your image as a generous and dedicated professional.

THE VALUE OF CONTINUOUS LEARNING THROUGH MENTORSHIP

While mentoring others highlights your leadership capabilities, embracing the role of a mentee reflects humility and a commitment to growth. In a rapidly evolving business landscape, seeking mentorship shows dedication to staying relevant and adaptable. Learning from others broadens your expertise, introduces fresh insights, and strengthens your brand.

As a mentee, you gain perspectives from mentors with diverse experiences or expertise. This exchange provides a holistic view of your industry and a broader skill set. Whether acquiring insights into emerging technologies or innovative leadership techniques, learning from a mentor underscores your willingness to evolve and improve.

Seeking mentorship also signals self-awareness and an understanding of your growth areas. Engaging with a mentor conveys resilience, adaptability, and a grounded approach to leadership—qualities that enhance your executive brand. By valuing learning and diverse perspectives, you position yourself as a well-rounded, forward-thinking leader.

CASE STUDY: HOW MENTORSHIP ENHANCED AN EXECUTIVE BRAND

Consider the case of a senior technology executive who mentored a young professional within her company. Through regular mentorship sessions, she guided her mentee through career challenges and shared insights from her own journey. Her mentorship became widely recognized within the organization, positioning her as an approachable leader invested in developing future talent.

Simultaneously, she sought guidance from a seasoned board member, who mentored her on corporate governance and strategic planning.

By engaging as both mentor and mentee, she cultivated a brand as a growth-oriented leader who values knowledge-sharing and continuous learning. This dual approach elevated her reputation both within her company and across the industry, showcasing her commitment to development, innovation, and responsible leadership.

PRACTICAL STEPS FOR ENGAGING IN MENTORSHIP

To maximize the impact of mentorship on your executive brand, consider the following steps:

Identify Opportunities to Mentor: Reach out to rising professionals in your network, whether within your organization or through industry groups, who may benefit from your guidance. Choose mentees with diverse backgrounds to expand your own perspectives and enrich your brand with broader insights.

Seek Out a Mentor: Identify mentors who bring expertise in areas where you want to grow. Engage mentors whose career paths align with your goals or who offer skills you wish to develop and approach them with specific objectives in mind.

Set Clear Goals for Each Mentorship Relationship: Whether as a mentor or mentee, define what you hope to achieve. For mentors, clarify the values and skills you want to impart; for mentees, outline the knowledge or guidance you seek. Establishing goals ensures both parties benefit and fosters a productive relationship.

Share Your Experiences Openly: Transparency in sharing both successes and challenges allows mentees to learn from your full journey, building a realistic view of leadership and reinforcing the authenticity of your brand.

Mentorship and Executive Branding

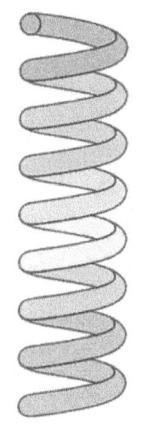

 Identify Opportunities to Mentor

 Seek Out a Mentor

 Set Clear Goals for Each mentorship Relationship

 Share Your Experience Openly

 Leverage Mentorship in Your Brand Narrative

Leverage Mentorship in Your Brand Narrative: Highlight your mentorship experiences on platforms like LinkedIn or in industry presentations. This reinforces your image as a leader committed to growth, generosity, and industry excellence.

Mentorship is a powerful tool in executive branding, providing a dual pathway for personal growth and professional reputation enhancement. By embracing the roles of both mentor and mentee, you strengthen your brand through demonstrated leadership, a commitment to lifelong learning, and authentic relationship building. Actively engaging in mentorship not only shapes a brand identity that is influential yet approachable but also positions you as someone who is grounded yet forward-thinking. Supporting the growth of others while seeking insights from seasoned professionals allows you to create a leadership legacy that transcends individual achievements. This approach firmly establishes your brand as one rooted in generosity, expertise, and an unwavering commitment to excellence within your industry.

UNLOCK THE MAGIC—
SCAN, TO LEARN MORE!

13
ALIGNING YOUR EXECUTIVE BRAND WITH CORPORATE CULTURE

For executives, an impactful personal brand seamlessly aligns with the culture, mission, and values of their organization. When your executive brand harmonizes with your company's ethos, it fosters cohesion, builds stakeholder trust, and reinforces the principles driving the organization's mission. This alignment creates a powerful synergy, enabling your personal brand to not only enhance your individual identity but also amplify the organization's goals and reputation.

In this chapter, we explore the importance of aligning your executive brand with corporate culture. We'll provide strategies to ensure consistency between your personal values and the organization's mission, reinforcing trust, credibility, and shared purpose. This alignment amplifies your leadership impact and strengthens the organization's brand identity.

WHY ALIGNING YOUR BRAND WITH CORPORATE CULTURE MATTERS

An executive's brand acts as an extension of the company's identity. When your personal values mirror those of the organization, you build credibility and deliver a cohesive message to employees, clients, and partners. Conversely, a misaligned brand can create confusion, erode trust, and introduce dissonance. For instance, an executive whose brand emphasizes innovation may struggle to connect with a company rooted in tradition and stability. By aligning your brand with corporate culture, you foster unity, serve as a model for employees, and reinforce the organization's mission authentically.

This alignment also enhances employee engagement and motivation. When employees see leaders embodying the company's values, it fosters trust and cultivates a shared sense of purpose. Your brand becomes a visible expression of the organization's mission, inspiring employees and reinforcing a culture where values are actively practiced. This connection creates a workplace where employees feel united with both their leaders and the company's broader mission.

Externally, aligning your executive brand with corporate culture strengthens perceptions among clients, partners, and investors. Stakeholders often look to leadership as a gauge of whether an organization truly lives by its stated values. An executive brand that consistently reflects corporate principles enhances the company's reputation, building stronger relationships and loyalty. Whether through public statements, media appearances, or corporate events, your brand serves as a representative of the organization's mission, projecting a cohesive and trustworthy image.

STRATEGIES FOR ALIGNING YOUR EXECUTIVE BRAND WITH CORPORATE CULTURE

Achieving seamless alignment between your personal brand and corporate culture requires self-awareness, intentionality, and a deep understanding of the company's core values. By aligning your actions, communications, and presence with the organization's mission, you strengthen both your personal and corporate identities.

1. DEFINE AND INTERNALIZE CORE VALUES

Start by gaining clarity on both your personal values and the organization's mission. Identify areas of overlap and use these as focal points for your brand.

Begin by reflecting on the principles that shape your leadership style, decision-making, and interactions. Are your values rooted in collaboration, integrity, innovation, or resilience? Once defined, compare them to your organization's core values. Most companies outline their values and mission in official statements, providing a blueprint for expected behaviors and attitudes. Recognize where your values align and reinforce them in your branding efforts.

For example, if sustainability is a key organizational value, incorporate this into your executive brand. Share thought leadership on sustainable practices, champion green initiatives within the company, and position yourself as an advocate for environmental stewardship. By embodying these values, your brand resonates both with your personal beliefs and the company's identity.

2. REFLECT COMPANY VALUES IN COMMUNICATION AND CONTENT

Your communication—whether in public speaking, meetings, or social media—reflects your brand. Ensure that your messaging consistently aligns with the organization's mission and values. When sharing content, connect it back to the company's purpose and use language that reinforces its ethos.

For instance, if transparency and ethics are core company values, emphasize honesty, accountability, and openness in your messaging. Transparent communication builds trust with employees and stakeholders, demonstrating your alignment with these principles. Frame your discussions around initiatives or trends in ways that highlight the values you wish to promote.

Incorporate corporate values into storytelling. Share anecdotes, lessons, or insights that underscore these principles. For example, if collaboration is a company priority, recount teamwork successes that highlight the importance of working together. Storytelling humanizes your brand, creating relatable connections with audiences who value authenticity and alignment.

3. MODEL VALUES THROUGH BEHAVIOR AND DECISION-MAKING

As an executive, your behavior and decisions profoundly influence perceptions of your brand. Align your actions with corporate values to reinforce the company's mission. Demonstrate the behaviors you expect from others, showing a commitment to the organization's principles.

For instance, if innovation is a key value, embrace new ideas, lead change initiatives, and celebrate team contributions to progress. Show that you are actively driving forward-thinking solutions. Similarly, when facing challenges, reflect the company's values by addressing conflicts openly, taking accountability, and acting with fairness. Modeling these behaviors strengthens the organization's culture and solidifies your brand as trustworthy and consistent.

4. ENGAGE IN COMPANY AND INDUSTRY INITIATIVES THAT REFLECT CORE VALUES

Participate in company-wide and industry-related initiatives that align with corporate values. This engagement demonstrates your investment in the company's vision and actively contributes to its realization.

For example, if corporate social responsibility is a priority, volunteer for community projects or support partnerships with non-profits. Attend or speak at events that reflect the organization's mission, such as sustainability forums or innovation conferences. These activities provide visibility and align your brand with initiatives that highlight the company's values on a larger platform.

Such participation also fosters connections with like-minded professionals, strengthening your network within the industry. These relationships further position you as a brand ambassador for the organization, reinforcing a unified and values-driven image.

THE IMPACT OF BRAND-CORPORATE ALIGNMENT ON CORPORATE COHESION

When an executive's personal brand aligns seamlessly with the corporate culture, it fosters a stronger sense of cohesion within the organization. Employees are more likely to feel connected and motivated when they observe leaders actively embodying the values that define the company's identity. This alignment creates a shared sense of purpose, signaling that the executive's personal values are not merely aspirational words but are consistently demonstrated through tangible actions.

Corporate cohesion extends beyond internal teams to include external stakeholders, such as clients, partners, and investors. A well-aligned executive brand reassures these stakeholders that the organization operates with integrity and consistency, reinforcing trust and fostering stronger, long-term relationships. When leaders consistently project values that align with the corporate culture, they communicate that the company is cohesive, principled, and reliable—qualities that significantly enhance its reputation within the industry.

CASE STUDY: ALIGNING EXECUTIVE BRAND WITH CORPORATE CULTURE

Consider an executive at a technology company where inclusivity and diversity are core values. To align their personal brand with this culture, the executive actively champions initiatives supporting diversity in hiring practices, team-building efforts, and professional development opportunities. They participate in industry panels on inclusive leadership, publish thought leadership articles on diversity topics, and use social media to celebrate team achievements in diversity initiatives. These actions create visible alignment between the executive's brand and the company's commitment to inclusivity, reinforcing the values that define the organization.

When employees witness their leader actively supporting diversity efforts, they feel inspired to engage with and uphold these values themselves. Externally, stakeholders perceive the executive as a true representative of the company's mission to promote inclusivity, which strengthens trust and enhances organizational credibility. By consistently demonstrating corporate values, the executive cultivates a personal brand that is both authentic and harmonious with the company's ethos.

PRACTICAL STEPS FOR ALIGNING YOUR BRAND WITH CORPORATE CULTURE

Achieving alignment between your executive brand and corporate culture requires intentional effort. Consider these actionable steps:

- **Regularly Revisit Corporate Values**: Stay informed about your organization's values and any updates to its mission or strategic goals. Adjust your personal brand accordingly to ensure consistency and relevance.
- **Engage in Cross-Departmental Collaborations**: Collaborate with teams across the organization to develop a holistic understanding of how corporate values are implemented at various levels. This comprehensive view strengthens your alignment with the company's culture.
- **Seek Feedback from Colleagues**: Ask for feedback from peers or mentors about how well your personal brand aligns with corporate culture. Their insights can help identify areas for improvement and ensure your efforts reinforce organizational cohesion.
- **Showcase Alignment Publicly**: Use public platforms, such as social media or speaking engagements, to share stories and examples that connect your personal values with the company's mission. This transparency reinforces your alignment and amplifies your message.

Aligning Executive brand with Corporate Culture

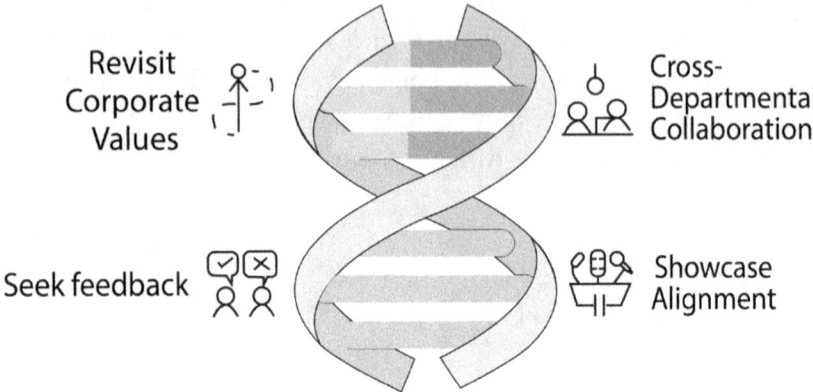

Aligning your executive brand with corporate culture is crucial for establishing a cohesive, trustworthy, and impactful leadership presence. When your personal values align with the organization's mission, it not only strengthens your brand but also enhances corporate cohesion, employee engagement, and stakeholder trust. By developing a brand that authentically reflects both your identity and the company's values, you create a powerful synergy that supports the organization's goals while bolstering your reputation as a credible, committed leader. As you embody the core values of your organization, you set a standard for others to follow, fostering a culture of integrity, purpose, and collective success.

UNLOCK THE MAGIC—
SCAN, TO LEARN MORE!

14

THE LONG-TERM MAINTENANCE OF AN EXECUTIVE BRAND

Building a strong executive brand is only the beginning; sustaining its relevance and impact over the long term requires deliberate effort, adaptability, and a commitment to growth. In an ever-evolving business landscape, executives who succeed in maintaining a compelling brand understand the importance of staying aligned with industry advancements. Long-term brand maintenance is about more than visibility—it's about remaining relevant, credible, and attuned to both industry shifts and personal growth.

In this chapter, we will outline strategies for sustaining your executive brand over time. By embracing continuous learning, adapting to industry changes, and periodically refreshing your brand to reflect new skills and accomplishments, you ensure that your brand remains both consistent and agile—reflecting your development while positioning you for future opportunities.

WHY LONG-TERM BRAND MAINTENANCE MATTERS

An executive's brand is a dynamic asset that reflects not only who they are today but also who they aspire to be. Without regular maintenance, even a strong brand risks becoming stagnant or irrelevant. A brand that doesn't evolve can quickly appear outdated or disconnected from current industry trends and personal achievements. Executives who actively maintain their brand continue to expand their influence, attract new opportunities, and showcase a leadership style that adapts to contemporary challenges.

Long-term brand maintenance also builds credibility and trust. Clients, colleagues, and industry peers view executives not only as experts but as adaptable visionaries who remain at the forefront of industry trends. By consistently evolving your brand, you demonstrate a commitment to growth, openness to change, and readiness to address emerging challenges.

KEY STRATEGIES FOR SUSTAINING AN EXECUTIVE BRAND

Sustaining an executive brand over the long term requires a combination of self-reflection, adaptability, and proactive engagement. By committing to continuous learning, refreshing your image, and refining your messaging, you can ensure your brand remains impactful and relevant.

1. EMBRACE CONTINUOUS LEARNING AND SKILL DEVELOPMENT

To keep your brand relevant, prioritize ongoing learning. Staying updated on industry trends, emerging technologies, and evolving market dynamics allows you to refine your expertise and incorporate current developments into your brand.

Identify growth areas within your industry and deepen your knowledge in these spaces—whether through formal courses, certifications, conferences, webinars, or professional groups. Expanding your skill set demonstrates a commitment to growth, enhancing your brand's credibility and relevance.

For example, if you're a finance executive observing a shift towards digital finance and blockchain, immersing yourself in these areas positions you as a forward-thinking leader. Sharing these insights with your organization or network reinforces your expertise in emerging areas, enhancing your brand's relevance.

2. REGULARLY AUDIT AND REFRESH YOUR BRAND IMAGE

As your career progresses, periodically assess your brand to ensure it accurately reflects your current role, achievements, and vision. Conduct a brand audit by reviewing how you present yourself across various channels—social media profiles, your website, public content, and your professional network—and make updates as needed.

Review key brand elements such as your mission statement, bio, and visual identity. Does your LinkedIn profile reflect your latest accomplishments and areas of focus? Are your photos and headlines aligned with the image you want to project? Small updates, such as revising your bio to include recent achievements or refreshing your profile picture, can significantly reinvigorate your brand.

Additionally, update your content to showcase new accomplishments and insights. If you've transitioned industries or assumed a more strategic role, refresh your narrative to reflect these changes. Actively shaping your brand helps avoid the risk of appearing stagnant or disconnected from your current goals and responsibilities.

3. ADAPT TO INDUSTRY CHANGES AND MARKET DYNAMICS

A well-maintained executive brand reflects an awareness of industry shifts and adapts accordingly. As new technologies, regulations, or societal issues emerge, adjust your brand to demonstrate insight into these trends. This positions you as a leader who remains informed and adaptable—qualities that are crucial for long-term success.

Stay engaged with industry publications, research studies, and thought leadership to track relevant changes. If your field undergoes significant transformation, consider repositioning your brand to highlight flexibility and expertise in navigating change. For instance, a healthcare executive might pivot to focus on digital health and patient-centered innovations if those trends become dominant in the industry.

Adaptability also means identifying elements of your brand that no longer align with your goals or the current landscape. Regularly reassess the values, skills, or messages associated with your brand to ensure they remain relevant. A brand that evolves with the times resonates more strongly with audiences, regardless of external changes.

4. UPDATE YOUR THOUGHT LEADERSHIP TO REFLECT NEW INSIGHTS AND INNOVATIONS

Thought leadership is a critical aspect of executive branding, and maintaining fresh, insightful perspectives strengthens your brand's impact over time. As your expertise deepens and new trends emerge, updating your thought leadership content ensures your insights remain valuable and timely.

Expand your topics to reflect new areas of focus. For instance, if you've shifted from operational management to digital transformation, share insights on technology-driven growth strategies. Thought leadership also highlights your journey of continuous learning, demonstrating your brand's agility and openness to new perspectives.

Regularly publish articles, participate in industry panels, or speak on podcasts to share updated insights and reinforce your brand's relevance. Consistent, timely thought leadership positions your brand as one that provides value to the industry, reinforcing your proactive approach to leadership.

5. CULTIVATE A GROWTH-ORIENTED NETWORK AND ENGAGE IN COMMUNITY BUILDING

Your professional network plays a significant role in sustaining your brand. By fostering a network that reflects both your achievements and aspirations, you ensure your connections are aligned with your brand's direction. Engaging in community-building efforts within your industry also strengthens your brand by demonstrating a commitment to collective growth.

Engage with emerging leaders, innovators, and established experts to maintain a dynamic, forward-looking network. Participating in community activities—such as industry events, mentorship programs, or professional organizations—demonstrates your dedication to nurturing talent and supporting industry progress. Expanding your network helps build a reputation as an executive who values collaboration and learning, which is essential for long-term brand maintenance.

Leverage your network for brand feedback and industry insights. Trusted colleagues or mentors can provide valuable perspectives on your brand's effectiveness and relevance, helping you refine your long-term strategy.

6. REMAIN AUTHENTIC AND ALIGNED WITH CORE VALUES

While adaptation and growth are essential, authenticity remains at the heart of a sustainable executive brand. In the rush to stay relevant, it can be tempting to pivot quickly or adopt trends that don't align with your core values. However, a brand grounded in authenticity stands the test of time.

Reflect on your foundational values and ensure they remain central to your brand as you evolve. Authenticity fosters trust, and a brand that consistently aligns with its core values—whether innovation, integrity, or inclusivity—will resonate deeply. By balancing adaptation with authenticity, you cultivate a brand that is both dynamic and rooted, generating lasting respect and credibility.

For example, if ethical leadership has always been a cornerstone of your brand, continue to champion this value through decisions, messaging, and interactions. Authenticity in these areas reinforces your credibility, making your brand resilient despite external changes.

CASE STUDY: MAINTAINING AN EVOLVING EXECUTIVE BRAND

Consider a tech executive who initially built their personal brand around operational excellence in software engineering. As their career progressed, they transitioned into strategic leadership roles, overseeing company-wide initiatives in digital transformation and AI implementation. To stay relevant, they updated their brand to reflect this new focus. This included sharing insights on the impact of AI on business growth, appearing on technology podcasts, and speaking at conferences on digital innovation.

At the same time, they continued to emphasize their commitment to ethics and transparency in technology—core values that had always been central to their brand. This authenticity, combined with a proactive approach to addressing emerging trends, allowed their brand to evolve alongside their career. By periodically refreshing their messaging, engaging with new content topics, and maintaining alignment with their core values, the executive built a brand that remains credible, relevant, and impactful.

PRACTICAL STEPS FOR LONG-TERM BRAND MAINTENANCE

Schedule Regular Brand Audits: Set aside time each year to assess whether your brand accurately reflects your current role, values, and achievements. Identify areas for improvement or updates.

Invest in Professional Development: Pursue learning opportunities aligned with industry trends or emerging skills, and incorporate these into your brand messaging to showcase growth.

Expand Thought Leadership Efforts: Regularly update your content and explore new topics that reflect the evolving landscape of your industry. Share your insights widely to reinforce your relevance.

Seek Feedback from Trusted Peers: Gain perspectives from colleagues, mentors, or industry experts who can offer constructive feedback on your brand's alignment and effectiveness.

Long-Term Brand Maintenance

Professional Development
Investing in learning to Integrate industry trends into brnd messaging.

Expanding content and Insights to maintain industry relevance.

Peer Feedback
Seeking constructive feedback to enhance brand effectiveness.

Brand Audits
Regular reviews to ensure brand alignment with current values and achievements.

Core Values
Staying true to fundamental principles for brand authenticity.

- **Stay Grounded in Core Values:** Adapt your brand as necessary, but always stay true to the core principles that define it. Authenticity is the foundation of a sustainable brand that endures.

Long-term brand maintenance is crucial for executives who wish to stay relevant and impactful in today's ever-evolving business environment. By embracing continuous learning, adapting to industry shifts, refreshing your brand image, and staying authentic, you can cultivate a resilient brand that evolves alongside your career. A well-maintained executive brand is not just a static identity; it's a dynamic reflection of your values, expertise, and commitment to ongoing professional growth. Over time, as you nurture this brand, you establish a lasting legacy of leadership and credibility that endures.

UNLOCK THE MAGIC—
SCAN, TO LEARN MORE!

FUTURE TRENDS IN EXECUTIVE BRANDING

The future of executive branding will be shaped by technological advancements, shifting workplace dynamics, and evolving stakeholder expectations. As new trends emerge, executives who proactively adapt will strengthen their brands and position themselves for long-term success. This chapter explores the key trends that will influence executive branding in the coming years, offering guidance on how to stay adaptable, leverage emerging tools, and remain relevant in an ever-changing business environment.

Today, executive branding goes beyond merely crafting a professional image; it's about building a responsive, forward-thinking presence that reflects an understanding of new challenges, technologies, and work styles. Leaders who embrace these changes can differentiate themselves, amplify their influence, and effectively communicate their vision in a digital, globally connected world.

THE IMPACT OF TECHNOLOGY ON EXECUTIVE BRANDING

Technological advancements are revolutionizing how executives build and manage their brands. From artificial intelligence (AI) to data analytics and digital communication tools, technology offers new ways to create, analyze, and optimize branding strategies. One of the most significant trends is the rise of AI, which enables executives to gain insights into audience preferences, engagement patterns, and content performance.

AI tools can analyze your digital footprint, suggest content topics aligned with industry trends, and monitor online mentions for reputation management. For instance, an AI-driven tool could assess your LinkedIn engagement, highlight successful topics, and recommend new themes based on emerging trends. Furthermore, AI supports reputation management by tracking brand mentions and facilitating timely responses to feedback or potential issues.

Virtual and augmented reality are also beginning to impact executive branding, particularly for leaders involved in public speaking, training, or remote team engagement. Virtual platforms allow executives to create immersive experiences, such as virtual keynotes or interactive webinars, fostering deeper connections with audiences. Integrating virtual reality into branding efforts helps executives stand out and showcases their commitment to innovation.

NAVIGATING THE REMOTE WORK ERA

The shift to remote work has transformed how executives connect with teams, peers, and clients, making virtual presence as important as in-person interactions. Leaders who excel in virtual communication and online relationship-building will maintain influence and visibility. Platforms like LinkedIn, Zoom, and Slack are essential for engagement. Executives can strengthen their brands by optimizing profiles, joining professional communities, and sharing thought leadership. Video content, such as updates or webinars, helps maintain personal connections. Trust and transparency are more crucial than ever. Leaders who adapt to virtual engagement will build accessible, adaptable brands that meet evolving workforce needs.

EMBRACING DIVERSITY, EQUITY, AND INCLUSION (DEI) AS CORE BRAND VALUES

As organizations prioritize diversity, equity, and inclusion (DEI), executives are expected to champion these principles. Integrating DEI into your executive brand demonstrates a commitment to a fair, inclusive workplace while enhancing brand appeal and relevance. To authentically embrace DEI, share your personal commitment and highlight actions promoting inclusivity, such as supporting diverse hiring, amplifying underrepresented voices, or fostering an inclusive culture. Engaging in DEI discussions positions you as a values-driven leader. By supporting DEI, executives build brands that resonate with diverse audiences and earn trust, ensuring long-term relevance in an increasingly socially conscious world.

THE RISE OF PERSONALIZATION AND HUMAN-CENTERED BRANDING

Today's audiences value authenticity and personalization from the leaders they follow. Human-centered branding encourages executives to connect by sharing personal stories, insights, and vulnerabilities, making their brand more relatable. Personalization also involves engaging directly through social media, responding to comments, and fostering two-way conversations. This builds trust and loyalty, making your brand feel approachable and empathetic. To enhance your brand further, tailor content for specific segments, addressing the unique challenges of each group. A personalized, audience-focused approach boosts relevance and influence across diverse demographics.

SUSTAINABILITY AND SOCIAL IMPACT AS BRAND DIFFERENTIATORS

In today's world, integrating sustainability and social impact into your brand can set you apart. Leaders who address environmental and social issues create purpose-driven brands that resonate with audiences who prioritize ethical practices. Share your sustainability efforts publicly, from green projects to social impact achievements. Advocate for change by participating in conferences, writing thought leadership articles, or supporting policies aligned with your values. Executives committed to sustainability build brands that are purpose-driven and forward-thinking, positioning you as a leader dedicated to the planet and society's well-being, qualities highly valued by stakeholders.

PROACTIVELY PREPARING FOR CRISIS MANAGEMENT

In today's business world, crisis management is key to executive branding. Leaders who handle challenges with transparency, resilience, and ethical decision-making enhance their brand's credibility. Future-focused executives must be ready for crises, whether from PR issues, regulatory shifts, or disruptions. Incorporating crisis management means staying calm and proactive, being transparent with stakeholders, admitting mistakes, and having a clear plan. Sharing lessons learned strengthens your brand's reliability, while a trusted network and communication channels ensure swift, effective responses when challenges arise.

Executives who proactively manage crises can turn challenges into opportunities to demonstrate leadership, reinforce their values, and build trust. A brand that incorporates a crisis-ready approach reflects foresight, adaptability, and a commitment to ethical leadership.

KEEPING YOUR EXECUTIVE BRAND AGILE AND FUTURE-FOCUSED

To maintain a strong executive brand in an ever-changing world, agility and adaptability are key. An effective brand strategy involves seeking feedback, staying informed about trends, and adjusting messaging when necessary. Regularly assessing your brand's relevance, embracing emerging trends, and exploring new platforms ensures responsiveness and forward-thinking. A future-focused brand embraces innovation, new technologies, and anticipates challenges. Positioning yourself as a visionary executive creates a brand that remains relevant today and resilient in the face of future shifts, signaling confidence and leadership regardless of market changes.

PRACTICAL STEPS TO EMBRACE FUTURE TRENDS IN EXECUTIVE BRANDING

Leverage Technology Wisely: Use AI-driven insights, data analytics, and other technological tools to enhance your brand strategy. Continuously explore new digital tools that help you monitor your brand's performance and adapt to evolving audience expectations.

Invest in Virtual Communication Skills: Develop your virtual presence by mastering video conferencing, digital presentations, and online engagement strategies. As remote work continues to grow, cultivating a strong virtual brand will become increasingly essential.

Incorporate DEI, Sustainability, and Social Impact: Authentically support initiatives in diversity, equity, inclusion (DEI), and sustainability. Make these core values central to your brand to resonate with modern audiences who prioritize social responsibility.

Adopt a Human-Centered Approach: Personalize your messaging and engage directly with your audience to build a more relatable brand. Share personal experiences, insights, and lessons learned to foster genuine connections.

Prepare for Crisis Situations: Anticipate potential challenges by developing a crisis management plan and building a network of trusted advisors. A well-prepared executive brand demonstrates resilience and integrity during times of uncertainty.

CONCLUSION: STAYING FUTURE-READY WITH A PROACTIVE BRAND

The future of executive branding will be shaped by leaders who adapt to change, embrace technology, and prioritize values like inclusivity, sustainability, and resilience. As technology evolves, workplace dynamics shift, and societal expectations grow, staying future-ready requires continuously refining your brand to meet new challenges and seize emerging opportunities. An executive brand that remains adaptable and aligned with these evolving values will resonate deeply with audiences.

By staying proactive, investing in new skills, and maintaining an authentic connection with your audience, you'll ensure your brand remains relevant and influential. A future-ready executive brand is resilient and visionary—capable of inspiring others and leading with purpose.

This chapter—and the book as a whole—offer a roadmap for building and sustaining an executive brand that thrives in an ever-changing world. Branding is a journey, evolving alongside your career and the world around you. Lead with clarity, authenticity, and adaptability, and you'll create a lasting legacy.

UNLOCK THE MAGIC—
SCAN, TO LEARN MORE!

16

TAKE ACTION TODAY - CRAFTING YOUR LEADERSHIP LEGACY THROUGH WRITING

You've explored the key elements of executive branding, discovered the power of sharing your story, and reflected on how your values shape your leadership journey. Now, it's time to take action. Writing compelling articles, thought pieces, or even a book can help you solidify your leadership philosophy, expand your influence, and leave a lasting legacy. The following steps will guide you in taking action today—developing impactful titles, integrating your values, and creating a body of work that authentically represents who you are and what you stand for.

1. DEVELOP TITLES THAT CAPTURE YOUR CORE MESSAGE

Begin with a clear purpose and audience in mind. Identify themes that define your leadership, such as resilience, innovation, ethical decision-making, or team empowerment. Consider the message you want to convey and how it aligns with your audience's needs, whether they seek inspiration, guidance, or stories of overcoming challenges. Use impactful action words like "transform" or "navigate" to spark curiosity and reflect your values. Keep titles concise yet powerful, ensuring they resonate and clearly express qualities like "authenticity" or "integrity" if these are central to your leadership style.

Take Action: Draft 5-10 potential titles based on your core themes. Use these examples as inspiration or create variations that align with your personal journey and leadership philosophy.

2. LET YOUR VALUES GUIDE THE NARRATIVE

Your personal values shape your unique leadership approach. Integrating them into your writing adds authenticity and depth. Start by identifying core values like integrity, empathy, accountability, or innovation, using them as the foundation for your articles. Share personal stories that showcase these values, offering readers insight into how they influence your actions and decisions. Frame each piece around a value-driven perspective. For example, begin with "Leading with resilience has taught me..." and build on that theme, offering actionable advice to help readers apply these values in their own lives.

Take Action: Reflect on a pivotal moment in your career where your values were put to the test. Write a brief outline for an article centered on this story, detailing the challenge, how your values guided your response, and the insights you gained.

3. WRITE WITH IMPACT USING SUGGESTED TITLES

Writing is an opportunity to express your unique voice and leadership philosophy. Choose titles that align with your story and use them as a springboard to explore your journey, beliefs, and approach to leadership. Here are 20 suggested titles to inspire you:

1. "Leading with Purpose: How Defining My Why Shaped My Leadership Journey"
2. "The Art of Resilient Leadership: Thriving Through Uncertainty"
3. "From Values to Vision: Building a Leadership Brand that Lasts"
4. "Embracing Change: Lessons on Adaptability in Leadership"
5. "The Power of Authentic Leadership: Why Being Yourself Matters"
6. "Transparency in Leadership: How Honesty Builds Trust and Loyalty"
7. "A Leader's Guide to Empathy: Connecting with Your Team for Greater Impact"
8. "How I Lead: 5 Core Beliefs that Guide My Decision-Making"

9. "Overcoming Imposter Syndrome: Embracing Confidence and Self-Belief"
10. "Leading by Example: Why Actions Speak Louder Than Words in Leadership"
11. "Building a Culture of Accountability: Lessons from My Leadership Journey"
12. "From Setbacks to Success: How Failure Became My Greatest Teacher"
13. "Innovation in Leadership: Fostering a Culture of Creativity and Growth"
14. "Navigating Crisis with Confidence: A Leader's Guide to Resilience"
15. "Servant Leadership in Action: Putting People First for Greater Success"
16. "How My Leadership Style Evolved: Reflections on Growth and Adaptation"
17. "Building Inclusive Teams: Embracing Diversity for Stronger Outcomes"
18. "The Power of Lifelong Learning: Why Leaders Should Never Stop Growing"
19. "Mentorship Matters: How Mentoring Shaped My Leadership Approach"
20. "Leading with Integrity: Staying True to Your Values Amidst Challenges"

These titles will allow you to share your leadership philosophy, challenges, and values. As you write, focus on delivering practical insights, relatable stories, and personal reflections that give readers a deeper understanding of who you are as a leader.

Take Action: Choose one title from the list and start drafting an article based on it. Outline your main points, integrate a personal story, and conclude with actionable takeaways for your readers.

4. SHARE AND AMPLIFY YOUR VOICE

Once your articles are complete, publish them on high-visibility platforms like LinkedIn or your website to amplify impact. Consistently sharing content strengthens your brand and positions you as a thought leader. Engage with feedback, adjust your approach, and keep delivering valuable insights to reinforce your executive presence.

Take Action: Publish your first article on LinkedIn or your preferred platform. Engage with your audience by responding to comments, sharing additional insights, and encouraging discussion around the topic.

UNLOCK THE MAGIC—
SCAN, TO LEARN MORE!

FINAL THOUGHTS: YOUR BRAND, YOUR LEGACY

Your leadership brand is defined not only by your actions but also by the stories you share, the values you uphold, and the insights you offer to others. By taking action today, you begin creating a body of work that reflects your unique journey and inspires future leaders. Each article you write adds a chapter to your legacy, establishing you as a leader of character, resilience, and vision.

Whether you're writing a single article or an entire book, remember that your words have the power to influence, uplift, and inspire change. As you craft your message, let your authentic voice shine through. Take that first step today—define your message, choose your titles, and begin your journey. Your leadership legacy awaits.

"A true leader's legacy isn't just in the milestones achieved, but in the values shared and the impact left on others. Lead with integrity, inspire through action, and let your brand be a beacon of growth and purpose." — Martin Rowinski

UNLOCK THE MAGIC— SCAN, TO LEARN MORE!

RECOMMENDED RESOURCES FOR EXECUTIVES

Expand your reach. Refine your brand.
Elevate your leadership.

As you close this book, remember — the journey *beyond the title* doesn't end here. It's only just beginning. The path to board leadership, industry impact, and lasting legacy demands both visibility and alignment. The following trusted resources will help you navigate your next step with clarity and confidence:

BOARDSI

(https://boardsi.com)

EXECUTIVE BOARD & ADVISORY OPPORTUNITIES + BRANDING SUITE

Boardsi is a trusted platform for connecting executives with board roles across industries. Whether you're pursuing your first advisory seat or expanding your board portfolio, Boardsi offers personalized support through its Board Suite and AI-powered matching system.

In addition, Boardsi's **Executive Branding Program**, powered by LEADAFI, helps position executives as thought leaders through professional bios, impact-driven articles, and consistent media visibility — giving companies and search committees what they need to say "yes."

ULTIMATE PUBLISHING HOUSE

THE ULTIMATE PERSONAL BRANDING TOOL? YOUR BOOK.

Want to elevate your credibility, attract more opportunities, and stand out as the go-to expert in your field?

Publishing a book isn't just a milestone — it's a *brand power move*.

At **Ultimate Publishing House**, we help entrepreneurs, professionals, and thought leaders become bestselling authors with a done-for-you process that works.

- Professional Ghostwriting & Editing
- Custom Cover & Interior Design
- Guaranteed Amazon Bestseller Campaign
- Global Distribution
- 100% Ownership of Your IP and more!

Your book becomes your business card, speaker tool, and legacy — all in one.

- **Call us toll-free: 1-833-I-LUV-BOOKS**
- www.UltimatePublishingHouse.com

Let's turn your story into a brand-building masterpiece

LEADAFI

(https://leadafi.com)

THOUGHT LEADERSHIP PUBLISHING FOR EXECUTIVES

LEADAFI (Leadership Authority & Influence) is a powerful executive publishing platform that turns your insights into industry-shaping content. Articles are distributed to thousands of decision-makers, building your digital footprint, credibility, and search authority. If you want to be found and followed, this is where to start.

7 WONDERS PODCAST

(https://www.7wonders.com/podcast)

LEADERSHIP THROUGH STRATEGIC STORYTELLING

Hosted by Emmy®-winning creatives, this podcast explores how top executives leverage storytelling to drive visibility, trust, and brand equity. Ideal for those who want to transform their narrative into influence that resonates across platforms.

BRAND ALCHEMY

(https://brandalchemy.io/)

EXECUTIVE BRANDING & VISIBILITY STRATEGY

A branding agency for high-performing executives ready to scale their influence. Brand Alchemy specializes in turning your career journey into a compelling brand narrative — across LinkedIn, media features, and board bios — so you're recognized before you're introduced.

GLDN PR

(https://www.gldnpr.com/)

MEDIA EXPOSURE & PUBLIC RELATIONS FOR ENTREPRENEURS & EXECUTIVES

GLDN PR helps executives and founders gain access to high-impact press, podcasts, and public appearances. Their curated media campaigns build reputation, trust, and exposure — without wasting time or budget.

GET PUBLISHED!

The Ultimate Publishing House's Production System is so precise, we can have your book released in 6 months:

All of our book publishing programs include:

- mastermind session
- personal project manager
- professional ghostwriter
- five phases of editing
- branded book website
- worldwide distribution
- marketing
- publicity
- media coaching
- book cover design
- image consulting

And much more!
UPH is here to make your book publishing dreams come true!

CALL TODAY TO START YOUR BOOK, IT IS THE BEST MARKETING INVESTMENT YOU WILL EVER MAKE!

647 883 1758 OR Email: author@ultimatepublishinghouse.com

The publishing world has changed dramatically. In the new economy with global opportunities, you are either distinct or extinct, the choice is yours.

A BOOK IS THE ULTIMATE BRANDING TOOL THAT OFFERS:

- Credibility
- Visibility
- Distinction
- Positions you as the expert in your field
- Media exposure
- Attract more clients or patients
- Opportunities for product endorsements
- It's time you publish your own book with the Ultimate Publishing House!

www.ultimatepublishinghouse.com

READY FOR WHAT'S NEXT?

Keep building. Keep showing up. Keep leading with purpose. Because your *title* doesn't define you — your *impact* does.

www.ingramcontent.com/pod-product-compliance
Lightning Source LLC
Chambersburg PA
CBHW060944230426
43665CB00015B/2052